What Others Are Saying About This Book:

Read this before you write your next book—it will streamline your activities.
—Travelwriter Marketletter

Creative people are more productive when they have the best tools. Get the best computer you can afford and this book.
—Sandy Whelchel, National Writers Association

Dan shares his experience and insights in a readable, clear and educational way.
—Ray Newton, National Coordinator
Reader's Digest Writing Workshops

I find the contents to be a treasury of wisdom, usable suggestions, and resource information that will be of much benefit to would-be authors. Its broad coverage also includes much that will appeal to old hands such as myself. I heartily recommend it.
—Nat Bodian, author, The Joy of Publishing

Dan is a genius in our business. Absorb his brilliance, wisdom, and re-duplicable insights by reading and employing this book. He'll show your how to profitably break into print and keep the money rollin' in.
—Mark Victor Hansen, Co-creator,
Chicken Soup for the Soul series

Busy people have trouble finding time to write. Savvy authors do several things at the same time. Dan Poynter shows you how.
—Hannelore Hahn, Founder and Executive Director,
International Women's Writing Guild

Writing Nonfiction is an invaluable, recommended addition to all personal, creative writing seminar, and public library writer reference collections.
—The Bookwatch

I'd trust Dan's word, recommendations and predictions over about any publisher, editor, agent or book marketing consultant I've met—and I've met the "supposed" best.
—Jay Abraham,
Getting Everything You Can out of All You've Got

This book offers the best tools and the best resources for becoming a successful writer.
—Maryanne Raphael, Writers World

I highly recommend this book to anyone who has a story but just can't imagine how to write it down.
—Bob Holt, Book Forum of San Diego

Dan is extremely generous with his time and the information he shares with his students, fellow authors and potential writers.
                        —**Alan Rothman, Sparetime Magazine**

Poynter is an insider. He knows the publishing business warts and all. He's practical.
                        —**Curtis Casewit, Books for Mature Adults**

Poynter's talent is to get writers motivated to get words on paper by showing them how to break down the project into palpable chunks, establish a schedule, and then bring all the parts together.
                        —**Laughing Bear Newsletter.**

Concentrating on the nonfiction book, Poynter takes you from selection of your subject through research, choosing your title and cover, to publishing choices.
                        —**Write Now! Magazine**

Every nonfiction writer needs a roadmap. Whether you are keyboarding or dictating, this book will guide your way.
                        —**Michael Larsen, Larsen-Pomada Literary Agency**

Every professional speaker needs to write a book for increased credibility and a passive-income source that keeps on giving. Dan's system is tailor-made for road-warrior speakers who can't seem to find the time to write.
                        —**Terry Paulson, Ph.D., past president,**
                        National Speakers Association

If I'd had this approach to writing when I was writing ads for electronic products and BluBlocker sunglasses, my life would have been a lot easier.
                        —**Joe Sugarman, president,**
                        JS&A/BluBlocker Corporation

Carefully researched, thoroughly documented, and well presented.
                        —**Cape Cod Writers' Conference Wave Length**

A handy, concise and informative sourcebook ... Expertly organized and chock full of hard facts, helpful hints, and pertinent illustrations ... Recommended for all libraries.
                        —**The Southeastern Librarian**

Writing Nonfiction

Turning Thoughts into Books

Dan Poynter

Fourth Edition, Completely Revised

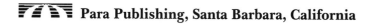 Para Publishing, Santa Barbara, California

Writing Nonfiction

Dan Poynter

Published by:

Para Publishing
Post Office Box 8206
Santa Barbara, CA 93118-8206, U.S.A.
info@paraPublishing.com; http://ParaPublishing.com

Copyright © 2000, 2001, 2003, 2005 by Dan Poynter.
4th edition, completely revised
Portions of this book previously appeared in *Write & Grow Rich*
Printed in the United States of America

ISBN Print Edition: 1-56860-110-7
ISBN Large Print Edition: 1-56860-116-6
ISBN PDF Screen Edition: 1-56860-111-5
ISBN PDF eBook Edition: 1-56860-122-0
ISBN LIT Edition: 1-56860-112-3
ISBN Palm Edition 1-56860-113-1
ISBN MobiPocket Edition 1-56860-114-X

Library of Congress Cataloging-in-Publication Data
Poynter, Dan.
    Writing   nonfiction: turning   thoughts   into   books   /

Dan Poynter 4th ed.
    p. cm.
    Includes bibliographical references and index.
    ISBN 1-56860-110-7
    1. Authorship. 2. Authorship—Marketing. I. Title.
    PN147   .P67   2005
        00-024842
    808'.02—dc21

    CIP

Contents

About the Author

Dan Poynter fell into publishing. He spent eight years researching a labor of love. Realizing that no publisher would be interested in a technical treatise on the parachute, he went directly to a printer. The orders poured in, and the author was suddenly a publisher.

In 1973, he became interested in a new aviation sport but couldn't find a book on the subject, so the skydiver and pilot sat down and wrote one. So far, *Hang Gliding* has sold more than 130,000 copies—a best seller!

Continuing to write, Dan has produced more than 120 books and revisions, some of which have been translated into Spanish, Japanese, British English, Russian and German. His books are loaded with facts and figures and detailed inside information. They are always up to date because he revises them before going back to press.

Dan is a pioneer. He wrote the first book on hang gliding, a circular book on Frisbee play and the first book on word processors. He published the first laser-typeset book in 1981. He was the first to send a galley to *Publishers Weekly* electronically in 1983. He embraced the fax in the mid-80s and pioneered fax-on-demand and to sell reports. He has been selling downloadable reports from his web site since 1996.

A consultant to the book industry, the Publishers Marketing Association recently presented him with the Benjamin Franklin Award for Lifetime Achievement. Dan is a past vice president of the PMA.

Dan is a frequent speaker (a Certified Speaking Professional) at writers' conferences and many other industry events. Dan runs his own publishing company, Para Publishing, in Santa Barbara.

Foreword

The book writing and publishing industries are in a state of accelerating evolutionary change. Publishing companies are growing and consolidating; emerging technologies are transporting information at the speed of light; the reservoir of text is growing ever larger; and the thirst for information is enormous.

The need for determined research and superior writing has never been greater. These industries require new ideas, new methods and new energies.

At the annual Maui Writers Conference, we have managed to bring writers, editors, agents and publishers together in an historic conspiracy to produce better books. Never before have these disparate groups worked together as they do in Maui (and then all year round).

Dan Poynter has subscribed to this new writing/publishing paradigm for years and now he reveals it to you in this book. When it comes to nonfiction, Dan is the top coach for writing, publishing and, most importantly, promoting.

Read this book now; start on your book today, and I look forward to seeing you in Maui.

John Tullius
Founder and Director,
Maui Writers Conference

Acknowledgments

I have not attempted to cite in the text all the authorities and sources consulted in the preparation of this book. To do so would require more space than is available. The list would include departments of the federal government, libraries, industrial institutions, Web sources and many individuals.

Valuable information (and inspiration) were contributed by David Beswick; Gordon Burgett; Charles "Stretch" Harris, Esq.; John Favot; Alan Gadney; Bill Frank; Susan Fulton; Dr. Bud Banis; Michael Kramer; Robin Kinkead; Rebecca Morgan; Stacy Peña of IBM Media Relations; Ellen Reid; Ruth Rose; Dan Seidman; Charles Kent, Esq.; and Joel Gould of Dragon Systems.

Melanie Rigney did the copy editing; Robert Howard provided another great cover design and Carolyn Porter did the design, typesetting and layout.

I sincerely thank all these fine people, and I know they are proud of their contributions to the book community as well as to this work.

A Word from the Author

Forget what you heard about book writing, publishing and promoting; the model just changed—for the better! Now you may print shorter runs at prices that make sense, publish your "books" in other (electronic) ways, sell them automatically and promote them for practically nothing. You will discover how to wring maximum value out of your work. This is an exciting time to be a writer.

To be successful, a book needs writing, design, production and promotion. I organized and automated some of these functions years ago. The last elements just recently fell into place to establish the New Book Model. You will love it!

There is not enough room in one manual to include everything that you should know about writing nonfiction. Consequently, Para Publishing has prepared many supplemental reports (called documents, special reports or instant reports) that are referenced in relevant places throughout this book. You may not want or need these supplements right now, but when you do, you can find them on our web site (See the section titled "A Complete List of our Products and Services" at http://parapublishing.com/getpage.cfm?file=products.html or by contacting us by email, telephone or fax.

I am also including numerous web site addresses for more information. If you are reading a downloadable edition of this book, you may click on the URLs and go directly to the sites.

My system works. In the back of *The Self-Publishing Manual,* I ask readers to send me their books once they publish. I receive 15 to 20 books each week.

Thank you for investing your time and money to allow me to share this new book-writing/production concept with you. I will make sure your time and money are well invested.

Dan Poynter, Santa Barbara.

Disclaimer

This book is designed to provide information about the subject matter covered. It is sold with the understanding that the publisher and authors are not engaged in rendering legal, accounting or other professional services. If legal or other expert assistance is required, the services of a competent professional should be sought.

It is not the purpose of this manual to reprint all the information that is otherwise available to authors and other creative people but to complement, amplify and supplement other texts. For more information, see the many references in the Appendix.

Book writing is not a get-rich-quick scheme. Anyone who decides to write a book must expect to invest a lot of time and effort without any guarantee of success. Books do not write themselves and they do not sell by themselves. People write and promote books.

Every effort has been made to make this book as complete and as accurate as possible. However, there may be mistakes both typographical and in content. Therefore, this text should be used only as a general guide and not as the ultimate source of writing and publishing information. Furthermore, this manual contains information on writing and publishing only up to the printing date.

The purpose of this manual is to educate and entertain. The authors and Para Publishing shall have neither liability nor responsibility to any person or entity with respect to any loss or damage caused or alleged to be caused directly or indirectly by the information contained in this book.

If you do not wish to be bound by the above, you may return this book to the publisher for a full refund.

Chapter One

What Your Book Will Do for You

Would you like to be recognized as someone who knows what he or she is talking about? Be someone worth listening to? Would you like to get paid for what you know? Would you like a job that is stimulating, interesting and challenging—a job you look forward to? Can you imagine doing what you love and loving what you do?

There are many justifications for writing a nonfiction book—fame, fortune, helping other people or fulfilling a personal mission. Let's take a look at each of these reasons.

Fame

Imagine being a published author. Picture people coming up to you at a meeting with a copy of your book and requesting an autograph. Visualize passing a bookstore and seeing your book in the window. Consider being interviewed for an article. Imagine the fame that comes with being published.

A book provides you with more credibility than anything else you could do: more credibility than for an audio CD, a video DVD, a seminar, a screenplay or a song. People place a higher value on a book—even though the same amount of work may have gone into the production of those other means of expression. The fact is that authors are highly valued in our society.

"Recognition is everything you write for; it's much more than money. You want your books to be valued. It's the basic aspiration of the serious writer."
—William Kennedy, novelist and Pulitzer Prize winner

People think that if you wrote a book, you know something. And you probably do. When you think about it, you are writing your book from the very best research plus personal experience. You will research relevant books and articles, distill their contents down to the essentials, direct your writing toward a specific audience and illustrate it with your personal experiences. You are earning an advanced degree in the subject by conducting the research and writing the paper. Your book validates your expertise and lends more credibility to what you say. You do "know something."

"Writing ranks among the top 10 percent of professions in terms of prestige."

—Jean Strouse, *Newsweek*

> I serve as an expert witness in skydiving cases. I am not a lawyer or an engineer and yet I advise attorneys, judges and juries what happened (or what should have happened) in parachute mishaps. My eight technical books on parachutes and popular books on skydiving give me the credibility to be hired and the credibility to be believed.

Once your book is published and you become an authority, your value and opportunities increase. You can charge more for seminars, articles, speeches and consulting. Imagine the credibility and recognition your book will bring you.

Radio/TV interviews. Every day, more than 10,200 guests appear on some 4,250 local news, interview and talk shows across the United States. And about 95 percent of the guests do not have recognizable names—yet.

Radio and television talk shows need interesting guests to attract listeners and viewers. Most people think that authors are experts and celebrities, so most of the guests booked on these shows are authors. Your book is actually your entrée to the airwaves.

Advertising products on the air is expensive and, since people are skeptical of advertising pitches, they usually tune them out. Interviews, however, are *editorial* matter. People listen to editorial matter. Interviews are more effective than advertising and they are free. They can be an inexpensive way to promote books.

"Many people love to go on radio and television. In fact, I think some people write books just to get on the air."

Autograph parties or book signings are a form of product promotion not open to producers of other goods or services. Bookstores, both chain and independent, are staging events to draw potential customers into their stores. Authors are the draw.

"Never do an autographing; always offer a mini-seminar. Attract buyers to your autograph parties."
                              —Terri Lonier, author, *Working Solo*

An autograph party says, "Come and appreciate me (and buy a book)," a seminar says, "Come on down and I will give you something free (information) that will improve your life." Always think of the *benefit* to the potential customer. How can you lure them out of the house and down to the store?

Patricia Bragg (Health-Science Publishing) publishes health and fitness books. To promote her mini-seminar at a local bookshop in Santa Barbara, she posted handbills in all the local health food stores. Then she made an emailing to her customer list within a 50-mile (driving) radius. The store was packed and she was "on" for more than four hours—until closing time. The store sold out on many of her titles and gave out rain checks. http://www.bragg.com

"For successful people, autographing scraps of paper for adoring fans is a duty. For authors, autographing (sold) books is money in the bank."

These mini-seminars may lead to more seminars or even a series of them for other groups at other locations.

"Books are a form of immortality. The words of men whose bodies are dust still live in their books."
                              —Wilfred A. Peterson, *The Art of Living by Day*

Fortune

Your book will be a new profit center. There is money to be made in books.

> It was a long flight home from the Maui Writers Conference and the guy in the next seat struck up a conversation. He finally got around to "And what do you do?"
>
> I sat up proudly and announced, "I'm a writer."
>
> "No, no," he quickly replied, "what do you do for a living?"

There are some starving writers out there, but most of them are working on fiction, entertainment that is more difficult to sell.

Fiction is a diversion and has to battle with other forms of entertainment for people's time. Fiction competes with reading other books, going to a movie or taking your kids to the zoo.

People are very short of time today. You can see them on the freeway trying to save time by driving, eating and talking on the cell phone—all at the same time.

Nonfiction is valuable information that people buy to save time or money. They are willing to pay you for the short-course in your subject and they will devote time to reading it. Worldwide, nonfiction outsells fiction by $55 billion to $25 billion.

Most publishers will urge you to work on your nonfiction first and to save your fiction until you can afford it. If you write nonfiction, put it in book form and publish it yourself, you can do very well.

"Fiction writers tend to be creative, interesting people who are fun at parties. But nonfiction writers drive better cars."

Many people are working on their own schedule, giving the world a piece of their mind and getting paid for it. This book concentrates on writing nonfiction, providing valuable information people want and need on how to do things.

"It is better to have a permanent income than to be fascinating."
—Oscar Wilde (1854-1900), Irish-born writer and wit

More business. A book makes you stand out. An author speaks with authority. A book brings customers to your door. Writing your book can be the cornerstone for a rewarding and successful future.

How much? But what does it cost to publish a book? That is like asking how much does a car cost. All books are different. But if you are planning to publish yourself and if you want to print 3,000 copies of a 144-page, 5½" x 8½" soft-cover book with a few photographs, black ink on white paper with a four-color cover, your printing and trucking bill will run about $1.55 each for a printing bill of $4,650. However, if you use short-run book production, a digital (toner) process, you can print and bind the same book in a quantity of 500 for $2.20 each, for a printing bill of $1,100. Or, you can print and bind 100 copies for $5.20 each, for a printing bill of $520. Per-unit prices depend on quantity, and prices fluctuate with the current price of paper (these are comparative figures not guaranteed prices). With digital printing, your per-unit price is higher but your invoice is less. Printing 500 books makes good economic sense for the initial run.

Then there is editing, typesetting (that many of us can do on our computers), book-cover design and other pre-press expenses. After the book is printed, it has to be promoted with book reviews, news releases and some direct email advertising. For a book like the one described above, you used to have to budget about $10,000 to get started. With the new writing, production and promoting techniques described in this book, you need just $1,500 to $3,000.

Your book could sell for $14.95 to $29.95, depending upon the audience. With this spread between production costs and selling price, you won't even mind giving the bookstore or other quantity buyer a 40 percent discount.

"Many first-time authors are not concerned about the money; they want the notoriety. They get smarter on their second book and look for the money."

On the other hand, if you decide to sell out to a publisher, you will get an advance against a royalty rather than invest your own funds. The details will be described later.

"Write out of love, write out of instinct, write out of reason ... but always for money."
—**Louis Untermeyer poet,
in *The New York Times*, September 30, 1975**

Personal Mission

Imagine being able to get the word out on something you feel strongly about.

> I love skydiving. I want to share it with the world; I want everyone to jump out of an airplane. Of course, I want you to make safe and enjoyable jumps so you will take up the sport, join the club, buy equipment and maybe even purchase some of my skydiving books.
>
> Since 1962, I have made more than 1,200 jumps. I have all the highest licenses and ratings and 12 hours of time (cumulative) in freefall. I am past chairman of the board of the U.S. Parachute Association and past president of the Parachute Industry Association.

When you have a sense of personal mission, your profit center is your passion center. Your vocation and avocation are the same. Why split your energies? Take a stand. Be passionate. Do not be afraid to stir up controversy. Picture sharing your enthusiasm with the rest of the world.

"Chase the passion, not the profit."
—**Terri Lonier, *Working Solo***

Helping others

Imagine helping others with a how-to book. Your years of experience could benefit a lot of people. Or, your memoir or story of personal triumph over adversity may change someone's life.

"We are all wounded. Our wounds are the single greatest source of material. Bad experiences make us experts on the subject. Talk about what worked for you. You have been there."
—**Dr. Susan Forward, author,** *Emotional Blackmail*

> Mindy Bingham was the executive director of the Girls Club of Santa Barbara. She realized that one-on-one, she could help dozens of girls each day. But if she took what she knew, added what she had learned, pulled documents from her files and did some more research, she could multiply her efforts and reach thousands. She wrote Choices, a Teen Woman's Journal for Self-awareness and Personal Planning selling more than a million copies so far. http://www.academininnovations.com/

So, you may be driven by fame, fortune, a personal mission or helping other people. If you are driven by fame, personal mission or helping others, the money will follow.

Seven Principles of Financial Success

1. There is more money in selling product than in selling hours. Most people sell their time; they are trading hours for dollars. Some people, such as doctors, charge a lot for their time, but they are still hourly workers. There are just eight or so salable hours in each day and then you have nothing more to sell. A product such as a book, on the other hand, is always working for you. It earns money even when you aren't on the clock.

Additionally, your book generates passive income. It produces revenue even when you aren't working.

> Brian Tracy is a well-known professional speaker who commands in the range of $20,000 per presentation. But these speeches also require a great deal of customized preparation time and lots of distant travel. For this reason, he has committed considerable time, energy and money to develop audios, videos and books that are sold through a variety of distribution channels. His goal is to achieve a 20-1 ratio of product to speaking, or 95 percent product to 5 percent hours. http://www.BrianTracy.com

2. There is more money in selling information about a product or service than there is in the product or service.

If you have ever attended a real estate seminar, you probably noticed the speaker was selling a book in the back of the room (BOR). What is ironic is that he probably made more money on the seminar and book than on real estate. And, once published, he became a lot more famous than he was selling real estate. In fact, you probably would not have attended the seminar if he did not have the fame the book brought him.

As a result of the seminar, you bought the wrong book. You did not need a book on real estate; you needed a book on how to write a book.

> I wrote the first book on hang gliding in 1973. Since I had a product for the industry, I attended meetings of the Hang Glider Manufacturers Association. One manufacturer observed that I was making more money than those who were bolting Dacron™ and aluminum together and more than the hang gliding instructors. I just smiled.

Pick any area of business and you will probably find that the consultants, authors and seminar leaders are making more money than the other business owners.

Information providers make more money than manufacturers.

3. Books reach more people. You can only help so many people with seminars, speeches and private consulting. Books are the most cost-effective way to multiply your efforts and bring your message to millions.

"Books are the carriers of civilization."
—**Barbara Tuchman, historian**
Authors' League Bulletin, **November 1, 1979**

You can consult with a small group of clients or speak to a roomful of attendees, but a book can serve far more people—on their own schedules.

4. A book is the ideal product because it is quick, fairly inexpensive and easy to manufacture. You can produce a lot more books just by letting the printing press run.

eBooks have even more advantages. They do not require printing, inventorying or shipping.

5. You control the product when you are its sole source. Do not invest time and money producing and promoting a product that interested buyers can buy from someone else (often for less).

> Joe Cossman was the originator and promoter of the Ant Farm, Spud Gun, Shrunken Head, Fly Cake and numerous other products. He would find local or imported products, nail down the source with a contract exclusive, have the products manufactured and then promote them. Joe said for years that if you are going to promote a product, you must be the sole source. http://www.cossman.com

If you control the product, you control the price. If you are not the sole (original) source, others will compete with you on the basis of price and the prices will decrease. It has been reported that 26 percent of book customers shop on the basis of price.

A manuscript can be copyrighted for only $30, giving you a legal monopoly to publish and sell it in any form you wish: hardcover book, audio, downloadable file, CD, foreign language, video, film, etc.

Books are a safe product; your copyright makes you the sole source.

6. As a publisher in today's environment, you can get paid sooner. Customers for many products are dealing directly with manufacturers. Dell does not assemble a computer until after it is sold and the company has received the money. In fact, Dell gets paid before it has to pay for the parts going into the computer.

Compare that model with Detroit. In that "on spec" model, the automobile manufacturers make cars and put them on lots. Dealers often sit on 60 days of inventory. It would make more sense to allow people to order a car online, pay for it, and get it built and delivered in two to three weeks—custom configured. The buzz phrase for this process is mass customization.

Traditional publishers follow the wrong model; they manufacture books on spec and place them in bookstores hoping someone will buy them. Unfortunately, 20 to 30 percent of the books are not sold; they are returned to the publishers for a refund.

With digital printing, we can print smaller quantities. Start with 500 and test the market.

7. You are your best investment. Do not spend time on frivolous activities or daydreaming. Each day, you are given 1,440 minutes. Put more of them to work. Invest in your future by using your time to write your book.

Subscribers to *Writer's Digest* magazine spend 12.64 hours writing each week. Beginners spend seven hours a week and advanced writers spend 30.5.

See "Finding Time to Write" in the writing chapter.

What Is a "Book"?

Today, a book has so many more forms than an ink-on-paper original edition. Your manuscript may become a hardcover book with a dust jacket, a perfect-bound soft-cover book, a mass-market paperback on wood-pulp paper or an audio CD; it may be downloaded and read on a computer screen; or it may be read on a PDA. Then it may be serialized, excerpted or condensed for magazines and ezines or translated into other languages.

Some people need your information but do not have time to read your book. They may commute lengthy, time-consuming distances each day. They would love to listen to your book to make double use of this time.

See the copyright page of this book for of all the editions in which it is available.

Take advantage of the new formats. Convert your text to other editions and wring maximum value out of your work.

How Long Will This Project Take?

Good book writing requires organization, discipline and application of the seat of the pants to the seat of the chair. Using the organizational plan outlined in this book will accelerate your writing process.

According to Brenner Information Group, on the average, authors take 475 hours to write books of fiction and 725 hours to write nonfiction.

> Terry Paulson, past president of the National Speakers Association, wrote the first draft of *50 Tips for Speaking Like a Pro* (Crisp Publications) using his laptop computer and speed typing during two long airline flights. Though it's a modest publication of just over 50 pages, and many of the quotations and other material already resided in existing articles in his computer, this is still a good example of speedwriting. http://www.terrypaulson.com

> Rick Evans wrote the 87-page *The Christmas Box* in six weeks. He published it and promoted it himself. It hit the top of the *Publishers Weekly* best-seller list and was translated into 13 languages. He subsequently sold out to Simon & Schuster for $4.2 million. http://www.RichardPaulEvans.com

> Years ago, I wrote the 168-page *Computer Selection Guide* in 21 days. Well, actually it took 28 days, but I carefully logged the time and found that during those 28 days the hours added up to 21 days of work on the book. Some of the material was adapted from an earlier work titled *Word Processors and Information Processing*. On the other hand, *The Parachute Manual*, my first book, took me eight years but *The Expert Witness Handbook* took six months because I enjoyed working on it so much. http://ParaPublishing.com

> Dianna Booher raises the bar even higher. She knocked out a 402-page book, *Communicate With Confidence!* (McGraw-Hill), in 22 days. *Get a Life Without Sacrificing Your Career* (McGraw-Hill) was first drafted over a long five-day weekend and *Would You Put That in Writing?* (Facts on File) took her four days. http://www.BooherConsultants.com

As you follow the plan in this book, you will qualify the project, assemble your materials and quantify the project. If you have done some writing previously or have recorded presentations that may be transcribed to writing, the whole process will be shortened.

"To write it, it took three months; to conceive it—three minutes; to collect the data in it—all my life."
—F. Scott Fitzgerald, *The Author's Apology*, a letter to the Booksellers' Convention, April 1920

To be realistic, your first book might take several weeks for organizing: gathering materials, setting up the binder, making the piles and doing the research. The first draft could take a week or two if you can set aside the time to marathon-write it. (We will discuss the drafts in more detail later.) The first draft is the toughest part for most writers. The second draft requires more research and could take several weeks. The third draft is for peer review and could take as long as three weeks. The fourth draft is the copy edit that you will probably farm out to a wordsmith. Meanwhile, you will be gathering quotations and stories, fact-checking statements and figures and soliciting endorsements and testimonials.

"I have never met an author who was sorry he or she wrote a book. They are only sorry they did not write it sooner."
—Sam Horn, *Tongue Fu!*

The Benefits of Being an Author

Authors have many advantages over those who do not write. Advanced communications allow the published author to live anywhere. All you need is access to a telephone line and the postal service. You can live anywhere; now you can reside where you like to vacation. While writing books requires organization and discipline, your schedule is up to you. You may drop anything at a moment's notice and travel when a good business opportunity arises. Best of all, this travel, your electronic toys and other expenses are deductible.

> I have been able to deduct my parachute jumps, flying lessons and aircraft rental. As part of my work, I have traveled to more than 40 countries and have even skydived into the North Pole.

Hazards of being an author. Your life changes once you become a published author. Authors are treated differently. Your status changes from that of a private person, the writer, to a public person, the authority. Some authors thrive on notoriety while others are reclusive and uncomfortable with it. If you treasure your privacy, your book will become a love-hate object.

"The author is the authority."

—Joe Vitale, *CyberWriting*

You may discover that people will think you are smarter than you really are. They will seek your advice on other subjects. Many people will just want to be near you. Some may even stalk you.

Writing your book should not be the end of your involvement. When readers have questions, authors have a responsibility to answer the mail and respond by telephone. Use these opportunities to gather material for the book's revision. Maybe you were not clear enough or perhaps the caller is interested in an important area you did not cover.

Your friends may also treat you differently once you have published a book. Some will be supportive and happy for you while others will be jealous because they didn't write the book. People new in your field will treat you like an idol while some of your peers will feel threatened and may be rather unkind.

> The difference between a blowhard and an author is that one has taken the time to put his views on paper. Both are telling you what is good for you, how to run your life. But one is a loudmouth you avoid at parties while the other is a gifted visionary you pay good money to read. The irony is that people may not want to hear what is good for them at the social function, but they will pay you $25 for the same information in a book.

Writing a book is a journey of discovery, an exploration and a learning experience. By planning, setting up our binder and drafting the back cover sales message, we set our sights on a path. But then, in the course of our writing and research, we discover new material, ideas and inspiration. The result is a finished manuscript that is different from what we originally projected. This book maps your journey.

Your future is up to you. Do not just hope for a bright future. Make a decision. Plan now, and soon you will be doing what you want to do. Your book will be the cornerstone for the future you are building.

Do not make excuses about lacking time. In these pages, I will show you how to skip over the unnecessary and to do two things at the same time.

Remember that writing is a solitary endeavor, so your book and your life are up to you—and only you.

📖

"Writing is not magic. But magic is not magic either."
—Bud Gardner, co-author,
Chicken Soup for the Writer's Soul

The Journey: From Idea to Published Book

1. Decide on an idea for your book.
2. Qualify the proposed book according to the *Six Musts*, found in Chapter Three.
3. Research the subject, title and competition.
   Check for other books (resources and competition).
   Stores, Amazon, Ingram.
   Check the possible title.
   Get a model book.
4. Select a working title.
5. Draft the back-cover sales copy.
6. Select a working title.
7. Set up your binder with dividers, front matter and back matter.
   Slip the mock-up of the covers into the outside pockets.
8. Assemble research materials into chapter piles.
   Research. Gather more content.
9. Decide whether you will *keyboard* &/or *dictate* your book.
10. First draft, rough draft. Get what you have into the binder. Draft all chapters before going back to edit.
    Add photos, drawings, quotations, stories.
11. Second draft. Content edit. Fill in the gaps.
12. Third draft. Peer review. Send out chapters for feedback.
13. Get testimonials for the back cover, front matter, etc.
14. Fourth draft. Copy edit. Clean up the punctuation, grammar and style.
15. Fact-checking. Confirm stories and facts. Confirm addresses and figures.
16. Decision:

Sell to publisher **or**	*Self-publish*
Get agent	Typesetting
Draft book proposal	
Sign with publisher	Proofreading
Proofreading	Printing

17. You are published!
18. Promotion: Send out review copies, make emailings, host autograph parties, give radio/TV interviews, etc.

"I never said writing your book would be easy. I only promised it would be worth it."

—Dan Poynter

Chapter Two

The New Book Model

This book you are holding is not just another tome on writing. It presents a completely new system that makes the product creation and production faster, easier and less expensive. If I could give just one thing to my fellow writers, it would be this New Book Model.

Today, the Web facilitates research, software accelerates typesetting, new machines automate printing and the Internet streamlines promotion. These technological improvements have spawned a fresh way to look at book publishing. The New Book Model covers all the bases and is a refreshingly innovative route for anyone with a manuscript.

Today, books are written in page-layout format using computer software. Then the pages are converted into Adobe Portable Document Format (PDF) for printing and conversion.

In the New Book Model, just 500 books are printed using computer-driven high-speed laser printers. The soft-cover and hardcover books are indistinguishable from traditional ink-printed books. Prices are just slightly higher, per unit, but the invoice is much lower.

PDF, LIT (short for Literature, the format for the MicrosoftReader eBook reader) and other files are generated for reading on eBook readers such as the Pocket PC.

Then, finished books are sent to two or three selected agents. A few more are sent to publishers with a track records for that type of book, an appropriate number are sent for review to genre-specific magazines, four or five are sent to specialized book clubs, about 10 are sent to foreign publishers suggesting translation and a handful are sent to opinion molders in the author's field.

If an agent or publisher comes in with a good offer, the author sells out. If not, all the bases are covered: the book is out for review and the orders are starting to come in.

Most of the book promotion is done via email; the author's web site replaces brochures. A press room on the web site replaces the media kit. For an example, see http://parapublishing.com/getpage.cfm?file=pressroom/pressroom.html. Avoiding printing and postage reduces promotion costs tremendously.

So, the New Book Model is a way to conserve time, inventory space and money while testing the market. More books are not printed until after they are sold. It is no longer necessary to tie up a lot of money and inventory in printed books.

This is *Information @ the speed of thought.*

"We have seen the future and it beeps. Welcome to digital book writing, publishing, promoting and reading."

Options for Producing Your Book

Today, there are choices when it comes to book production.

Traditional offset printing (ink on bound paper). Putting a lot of ink on paper is now just an option. It is a good choice if there is a large prepublication demand such as advance sales to bookstores or a quantity sale to a book club. Otherwise, there is no need to print 3,000 or more copies of your book to achieve acceptable economies of scale. In the future, most books will not be manufactured until *after* they are sold.

Offset printing is a quantity game. The more books you print, the lower the per-unit price. To reduce the cost you want to print more, but not so many that you will have books left over when demand slackens.

There are about 40 offset book printers across the United States and Canada. While any printer can produce books, only those that specialize in books can deliver price, service and quality. For a list of those printers, see the Appendix.

Digital book production uses a higher speed direct-to-image (drum) electrostatic process with a toner blend that reproduces photographs well. There is no film or plate. The process is cost effective for quantities from 100 to 1,500 copies. Color covers may be printed with toner, digital ink or the traditional offset ink process.

With digital printing, each book can be customized. Pages can be substituted and cover art can be changed. If you make a premium sale to a company, you can add an introductory page from the CEO and/or include the business' logo on the cover.

A Typical Digital Printing Plant

A digital printing plant is quiet and clean and uses lower-cost equipment than a traditional offset facility. Digital printing is cost effective to 1,500 copies.

Normal trim sizes for digital printers are 5.5" x 8.5," 8.5" x 11," 6" x 9" and 7" x 10." The most economical are 5.25" x 8.25" and 8.25" x 10.75."

Delivery is typically five days from page proofs (blue lines), and reprints should take two to three days.

Book distributors may one day install short-run machines to make books as ordered by the stores. Then publishers will send PDF files instead of pallets of printed books to distributors.

Short-run book production offers lower investment costs, reduction in inventory, custom publishing, quicker reprints and elimination of obsolescence.

For a list of digital printers in the United States and Canada, see the Appendix.

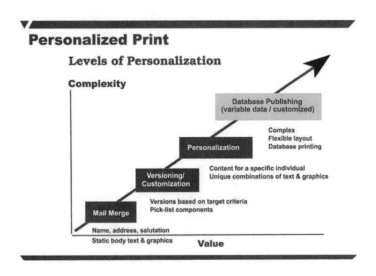

Personalized Print

Levels of Personalization

The chart shows the various levels of personalization available today. It starts at the bottom of the value chain with simple Mail Merge capabilities. This is the lowest level of personalization because the body of the book remains the same. The next level is versioning or customization. This higher level of personalization allows selected books to be target to specific readers. Typically the author prints multiple copies of a versioned book for the target. For instance, one version of the same book may be dedicated to bankers while another version of the same book may be dedicated to real estate salespeople. The third level is called Personalization. In this stage, a unique book is created for each unique reader. The fourth, and final, stage of personalization is Database Publishing. In this stage, each book is entirely unique. Chapters, charts, layouts can vary for each unique reader.

As one moves up the ladder of personalization, the complexity of printing increases dramatically. To print a personalized book is more expensive than a generic book. At the same time, it should also command a higher price because it is specifically targeted at the reader.

Print on demand (POD) is not a method of printing but a way of doing business. It means making a book to order. Most POD book manufacturing is done with digital presses. Making books one at a time is more expensive per unit than printing a small run.

One major POD printer also offers access to bookstores. Contact Lightning Source/Ingram for details. http://www.lightningsource.com.

"POD is not new. Those monks who were hand-lettering manuscripts in the abbeys were doing print–on-demand. They received an order for a book and they made one."

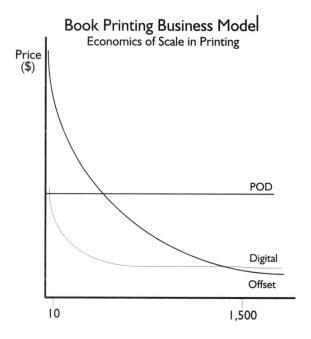

Book Printing Business Model
Economics of Scale in Printing

Comparative Costs

Comparing costs. As you can see on the chart, offset printing requires a lot of set-up time. Print Quantity Needed (PQN) or digital printing requires little set-up time, but the machines run much more slowly.

Because of the set-up time, offset printing requires at least 3,000 copies to achieve a reasonable per-unit price. Digital PQN printing can be done in smaller quantities at a reasonable price, but remember that you will need 500 books to send out for review and other promotion. POD costs much more per unit; too much for promotional purposes.

Covers. Most books are manufactured with soft covers called "perfect binding." In traditional printing, hard or "case" binding runs about $1 extra per book. For short-run digital production, the cost is $3 to $4 each, depending on the thickness of the book. For individual POD copies, the cost for case binding is often higher.

Once your manuscript is in PDF, copies can be printed out on a laser printer and installed in preexisting hard covers. See http://www.channelbind.com. These hard covers can be im printed (gold stamped) or you can wrap a jacket around them.

eBooks. While this information about ink-on-paper publishing is important, the electronic edition of your book will be far more useful to your reader. In addition to being searchable and less expensive, all the referenced web sites will be hyperlinked. Readers of the electronic edition can just click on the reference and go to the linked web site.

To save money on book printing, many of the larger publishers have resorted to smaller type, reduced leading (space between the lines of type) and narrower margins, resulting in a wider text block. The books are more difficult to read. The type size in an eBook, however, can be adjusted to suit the reader.

The only ink-on-paper ("dead tree") books in the future will be coffee table books—books as an art form. These books will be used to decorate homes and offices. Other information will be disseminated electronically without sacrificing trees.

"Publishing ink on paper is going to become a mere service to readers. The real product we're going to sell is the digital product."
—**Bruno de Sa Moreira,** *Zeroheure* **magazine**

Living in the Communication Age

People need more information to make critical decisions, and they want that information quickly. As an author, you have the information some of them need, and you can get it to them faster electronically than through traditional hand or postal delivery.

We are not just in the information age; we are in the electronic information age or, better yet, the communication age. Fortunately, authors deal in products that can be communicated. The knowledge world is going from a paper culture to an electronic culture. It is only a question of how we want to package our information.

"If book publishers can't see the writing on the wall, it's because the writing is not on the wall. It's on a computer screen."

Historically, a book had to be published in hardcover to be taken seriously by the media. In a few years, a book still will have to be in paper form (as well as digital) to be considered successful. A printed-paper edition will signify that the book is selling well enough to justify an ink printing. **The costs of electronic delivery** of information are decreasing while the costs of physical storage and delivery are increasing. That is why the fax became an everyday machine. We have learned it does not pay to give someone a letter, 37 cents and several days to hand carry the message across the country. Email will do it faster and cheaper.

Compare cost v. speed. US Mail service costs 37¢ and takes several days to deliver. FedEx costs $12.95 for an overnight letter and arrives the next day. Faxes cost between 10¢ and 50¢ per minute and it takes 3 minutes per page of material. E-mail is virtually free and arrives instantaneously. People want and need their information faster and sooner today.

No middleman. Disintermediation is a marketing buzzword; it means cutting out the intermediaries such as publishers, distributors, wholesalers, bookstores and printers so that customers can deal directly with manufacturers. In our case, that means readers buying directly from authors.

By cutting out the person in the middle of the transaction, we can sell the written product for less and still make more money while the customer get the information sooner.

"The breakthroughs are leading authors to bypass publishers, to become publishers and bookstores to become retailers."
—Don Clark in *The Wall Street Journal*

Release 1.1. Since you are not investing in thousands of printed books, you do not even have to finish writing the nonfiction book to sell it. You can post a chapter or two on your web site and invite feedback. Then as you add to the "book," you can post new versions as 2.0, 3.0 and so on, and sell to the same customers again.

Traditionally, books are published as one-shot, one-season (four-month) projects. If the book sells well, it is reprinted. If it does not, it is pulled from the shelves. This system makes sense for fiction (entertainment) that will not be updated. It is not logical for nonfiction (information). Savvy publishers have been updating their nonfiction and publishing revised editions for years.

Electronic editions can even contain a pop-up message inviting the reader to click on a hyperlink to the author's web site to see if there is a new edition. Now you can remind the reader over and over again—even if a friend loaned the eBook.

Module books. Books can have several versions of some chapters, each aimed at a particular type of reader. Then the book can be assembled for that particular reader. The customer might be asked some basic questions: What is the level of your experience? Are you new to the subject, familiar with it or an expert? Where are you located? (Your approach to a market may be different if you are outside the United States.) In what language do you want the book? Then the program would select various versions of the chapters or modules and assemble them into a "book" to meet the needs of the buyer.

ebook readers (hardware) provide info-to-go; they make the electronic information portable. You can make your entire book available for eBooks in PDF and other formats. Here are the major players. See their web sites for details.

Hardware for eBooks

Pocket PC.
http://www.microsoft.com/windowsmobile/products/pocket pc/default.mspx

Pocket PC

Palm, Inc.
http://www.palm.com/us/
This Pocket PC stores thousands of books; the capacity depends on the inserted storage card. The text is one newspaper-column wide and the display is backlighted for reading in the dark. It stores your calendar and address book and synchronizes with your desktop PC. The one pictured even has a cell phone for calls and mobile email.

Software for eBooks

- 📖 Pocket PC, MS-Reader, LIT files.
  http://www.microsoft.com/reader/default.asp
- 📖 Adobe Acrobat PDF
  http://www.adobe.com/epaper/ebooks/main.html
- 📖 Palm Digital Media
  http://www.palmdigitalmedia.com/REFID=42122/home.cgi
- 📖 MobiPocket
  http://www.mobipocket.com/en/HomePage/default.asp

"By 2020, fifty percent of everything we read will be in electronic form."

—Dick Brass, Microsoft vice-president in charge of technology development

Downloadable virtual books allow you to write, store, sell and read your work without printing it out.

eBooks are not for everyone. If you spend a lot of time at home, pBooks (printed) work fine. If you are a commuter, sales rep or long-haul trucker, you may prefer aBooks (audio). If you travel and spend a lot of time on airplanes and in airports, eBooks offer a low-weight, low-volume alternative to pBooks.

Distribution: your web site. You can put the entire book on your own web site for downloading. For example, Para Publishing sells 48 unlockable reports. You can read them or print them out. See http://www.parapub.com/getpage.cfm?file=products.html

Sample read. If you write fiction, place the first chapter of your book on your site as a free read. The first chapter is usually full of action and encourages readers to continue. If you publish nonfiction, place the first page of *each* chapter on your site as a free read. In nonfiction, you are selling information, not entertainment. You will convert more browsers into buyers if you introduce them to the material in each chapter.

Distribution: other web sites. You can put the entire book on other web sites for sale and downloading. Since these sites are proliferating at a great rate and because their offerings are constantly evolving, minimal information is given below. See the sites for more information.

Amazon.com. You can sell almost anything utilizing Amazon's one-click ordering. http://www.amazon.com/

Barnes & Noble.com. http://barnesandnoble.com

BookLocker sells downloadable books in PDF format. http://www.booklocker.com

CyclopsMedia. http://www.cyclopsmedia.com/v4/index.html

OfficeMax. http://www.ebooks.officemax.com/

NetLibrary sells downloadable books to consumers and libraries. http://www.netlibrary.com

These are the major players. For more retailers and the latest details, see our Document 615, pBooks to eBooks at http://www.parapub.com/getpage.cfm?file=products.html. You do not need this information now.

Entertainment		Information
Music	**Fiction**	**Nonfiction**
Appeals to many	Appeals to some	Appeals to few
Used repeatedly	Used once	Kept as reference
Often shared	Occasionally shared	Rarely shared
Not revised	Not revised	Revisable
Multi-task	Single task	Single task

"Today, there are only two types of publishers: those in danger of missing the electronic boat and those who do not even know there is a boat to catch."

Digital Rights Management (DRM)

Hearing about the effects of Napster on music proliferation, some people are concerned about making their books available for download. But music and even fiction have much wider audiences than subject-specific nonfiction. Nonfiction is less likely to be distributed to others.

Protection schemes penalize paying customers and create additional customer service costs. Weigh the value.

eBook procedure. There are four easy steps to selling our book at Amazon and other eBook download sites.

1. Write your book in MS-*Word*.

2. Send the file to http://www.RosettaMachine.com. Your work can be converted into four eBook formats for $350 or $997, depending on the plan.

3. Submit the converted files to http://www.LightningSo urce.com. Lightning Source is a division of Ingram, the largest pBook wholesaler.

4. Ingram will post your books at Amazon.com, Borders.com, CyclopsMedia, OfficeMax, BookLocker, Palm, MobiPocket, Yahoo!, Powells.com, et al. Ingram takes 55 percent of the sale and gives the retailer a discount. Your up front costs are just a few hundred dollars; after that, you only pay a "commission" on sales. Ingram collects from the retailers and sends you a check each month.

For a list of other content conversion providers, see http://www.microsoft.com/readerpartners/conversionpro viders.asp

More Delivery Options for Your Book

CD-Rom. You can make up a few CDs so those who prefer the CD or do not have broadband Internet access can play your book on computers. Include the free Adobe Acrobat Reader on the CD for those who do not have it loaded on their machine. Your CD edition will be searchable, have live hyperlinks and so on. You could even add motion and sound.

For small-quantity CD duplication, see details and pricing at http://www.natlcass.com. List the CD with online bookstores that are not set up for the downloadable version.

Audiobooks. Once your text is on disk, you have a script for your aBook. Some of your potential clients do not have time to read your book, but would like to listen to it while driving.

"Spoken-word audio turns your car into a university."

—Judith Sinclair

Downloadable files will soon replace spoken-word audiotapes and CDs. See the following web sites:

http://www.audible.com

http://www.riohome.com/

http://www.nomadworld.com

http://www.salon.com/audio/index.html

For the latest information on aBooks, see Document 635 AudioBooks; Turning Books & Speeches into Spoken-Word Disc & Download Products. See http://www.parapub.com/getpage.cfm?file=products.html You do not need this information now.

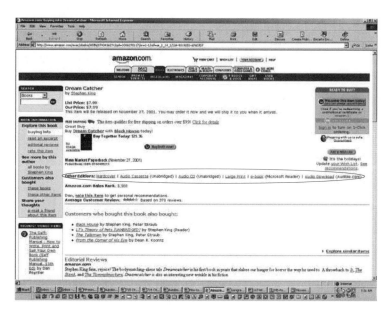

Provide a choice of formats

YOUR PUBLISHING SEQUENCE

☐ Follow the New Book Model and print 500 copies digitally. The books will establish your credibility and will serve as the foundation for your business.

☐ Then send your MS-Word file to RosettaMach ine.com and LightningSource.com. This is easy because the file is already done.

☐ Next, record the aBook. This is easy because the book is the script; it is nearly done

Be aware that each edition of your book—paper, download, audio, etc.—must have a unique International Book Standard Number (ISBN) to differentiate it from the other editions. See the ISBN discussion later in this book and visit http://www.ISBN.org.

The New Book Model is easier, faster and less expensive than models of the past and will bring authors a greater return. You *can* do it yourself. You can make more money, get to press sooner and keep control of your work. You can repurpose or multipurpose your content, publish it in several different ways and wring maximum value out of your literary effort.

In the future, nonfiction book publishing will see minimized inventories and maximized relationships between authors and customers (readers). Publishing will become customer-centric and "books" will thrive on uniqueness, customization and variety. Book writing and publishing is changing—for the better.

📖

Chapter Three

What to Write: Selecting Your Subject

You may write anything you wish. The First Amendment to the Constitution guarantees freedom of expression. In the United States, you do not have to register, get a license or ask permission to be an author.

Making the decision. Use the following criteria-the Six Musts-to qualify your project. If you have already written the manuscript, go back and make sure it meets all six of them. Unfortunately, many authors write before considering the Six Musts, and then they discover there aren't any potential buyers for their book.

> I never know what book I will write next; I do not plan ahead. An article, a few words from a friend or an activity may trigger an idea. I visualize the book, check it against the Six Musts and make a decision.

"The best time for planning a book is while you're doing the dishes."
—Agatha Christie, English mystery writer

The Six Musts for a Viable Book

1. The subject must be interesting to you. Write what you know. What are your interests? Plan your future and your book now.

Do not write a book on a subject that you are no longer interested in and do not want to pursue. For example, let's say you have been selling real estate for the past 10 years, but your hobby is golf and you are pretty good at the game. Do not write on real estate; write it on some aspect of golf. Once your book is published, people may request interviews, articles, seminars and consulting. Plan now to make sure they approach you on a subject about which you are passionate. Follow your heart, not your head.

Ask yourself: What do you want to be writing about in three years? What do you want to be talking about? What do you want to be dreaming about? What will wake you at three in the morning with a burning inspiration that will move you to the keyboard?

"My object in living is to unite my avocation and my vocation."
—Robert Frost (1874-1963), American poet,
Tramps in Mudtime

Ask yourself: Is this the *subject* I want to focus on?

2. You must have expertise or experience. You do not have to have an advanced degree; you do not need a Ph.D. But you do need personal experience, dedication to do research and a deep desire to spread the word. The most important question is "Have you been there?"

"You must have experience to write a good nonfiction book, so please do not write a book on *how to get rich* unless you are already rich."
—Patricia Clay, actor

A study published in the *Journal of the American Medical Association* in 1999 found that people who wrote about their traumatic life experiences sometimes gained relief from chronic asthma, rheumatoid arthritis and other diseases. Those who spent just 20 minutes per day, three days in a row, writing about the most stressful event in their life were in better health four months later than those who did not. Apparently, writing had a therapeutic affect, helping them make sense of their bad experiences.

A fresh outlook can be an asset. When you are beginning in a new field, you have the same questions your readers will have. Write as you learn and record as you study. Then run your manuscript by more experienced people to make sure you have not left anything out or written something you misunderstood. This process, called "peer review," will be covered in the writing chapter.

I became interested in the new sport of hang gliding in 1973. Being book-oriented, I visited the bookstores and the library. Unable to find a book on the subject, I wrote one as I learned to fly. I sent finished chapters to instructors and manufacturers for review. This first book on the sport sold so well that I was able to move from New England back to California and buy a home in Santa Barbara.

Ask yourself: Do I know what I am talking about?

3. The subject must be of interest to others. The book has to contain information people want to know or they will not buy it. Will a number of people be willing to part with a twenty-dollar bill to lay their hands on this book? Will it sell?

Ask yourself: If I build it, will they come?

4. The subject must be tightly focused. We live in an age of increasing specialization. Years ago, we had general, weekly magazines, periodicals such as *Collier's* and *Look*. They are gone now because people do not have time for or want a general magazine. Today, they read *Writer's Digest*, *Publishers Weekly*, *Graphic Arts Monthly* and *Parachutist* magazine. Target your information, your message and your audience. Narrower is better.

Marilyn Grams attended one of our first book-promotion workshops. A medical doctor, Marilyn had recently given birth to her second child, and had just finished her manuscript on breastfeeding. Mindy Bingham asked her who her intended reading audience might be. Marilyn thought the answer was rather obvious: any woman who had given birth or who was about to give birth and is interested in breastfeeding. Mindy reminded Marilyn that she had developed a system whereby a woman could breastfeed and return to work. She suggested the book be titled *Breastfeeding Success for Working Mothers*. Marilyn did not want to limit her market; she wanted to sell to all new mothers. Mindy said, "Let's pretend we are in a bookstore looking for a breastfeeding book. There are eight books on the subject." Then Mindy, who has a mind like a steel trap and has never forgotten a statistic she has ever read, said, "Marilyn, do you know that 55 percent of the women who give birth return to the workforce within one year?" That meant that 55 percent

> of the potential buyers would identify with *Breastfeeding Success for Working Mothers* and the other 45 percent would spread their buying over eight books. Narrowing a book's focus means more buyers will identify with and purchase it.

Women purchase 68 percent of all trade books. If you aim your message at women, a great majority of the potential buyers will *identify* with your book. For example, it only took *Chicken Soup for the Woman's Soul* six months to sell as many copies as the original Chicken Soup for the Soul sold in its first three years. Women will listen to women talking about women's issues.

Ask yourself: Is the subject of my book narrow enough?

5. The market must be easy to reach. Who are your readers and where are they? You must be able to **identify** them and *locate* them. Remember that your answers are not "book readers" in "bookstores".

Go into a bookstore on any given day. How many of the customers do you suppose are interested in a skydiving book? Not many. What is the profile of the typical bookstore browser? It is the recreational reader, someone used to plunking down $24.95 for hardcover fiction. But check out a parachute shop. How many customers are interested in skydiving? Now the thinking gears are turning. Where can we find a high concentration of our particular customer? What type of stores do our potential customers frequent? What magazines do they read? What associations do they join and what events do they attend? Go where the customers are.

For example, skydiving books are sold through parachute stores, skydiving catalogs and skydiving schools as well as to the U.S. Parachute Association for resale to its members. Reaching buyers is easier and less expensive when you identify a high concentration of them.

Specialty dealers purchase books by the carton, feel a 40 percent discount is generous, pay in 30 days and never return a book. Bookstores, in contrast, buy two or three books, complain about the discount, might pay in 90 or 120 days and then return one book for a refund. And, often it is damaged with coffee stains. Bookstores are lousy places to sell books.

Ask yourself: Do I know where my potential customers are?

6. The market must be large enough (but not too large). The primary group you are targeting should be between 200,000 and 700,000 identifiable, reachable people. To get these figures, check the number of stores that target your potential customer, the membership of applicable associations and clubs, the subscriber count of appropriate periodicals and the turnout for events they might attend. If the group is too small, you won't sell enough books to quit your day job. If it is too large, you will have competition. In large groups, you will have to narrow your target even more. For example, there may be 10 million water skiers. How about a book aimed at water-skiing instructors?

Eventually, you will want a line of books, audios, disks, seminars and speeches, all covering the same subject. These products and services will fill up your website "brochure". Then you will become known as the central source for all information on your subject.

"You are not just an author, publisher, publicist, speaker or consultant. You are an *information provider*."

Ask yourself: Is my projected audience large enough to support me?

Does your subject qualify under the Six Musts? If you satisfy the six criteria, you are on your way.

"If it doesn't work, begin something else."
—Bernard Malamud (1914-1986),
American novelist and short-story writer

Building Your Business

Your book is the foundation for your business. The other products and services are built on top of the book. The book must come first as it provides more credibility than any other product. Don't spend time making an audio just because you can turn it out faster. Do the book first.

Stay in one field. Once you select your subject, stick to it; stay in one field. Many authors write a book on a subject they know quite well and direct it to their own, reachable field. The book becomes a success using this formula and they suddenly think that selling books is easy, so they write a travel book. It flops because they do not know how to reach the travel-book buyer.

One day, I received a call from a client. He said, "I am a chiropractor, and I recognize that while chiropractors are good at what they do, they are not good at running their offices. But I have solved that challenge. I have just finished my book titled *How to Run Your Chiropractic Office.*"

"Sounds good," I said. I thought to myself: "Now here is an author who can look into the mirror and see a reflection of his customer. He knows who the customer is, what the customer needs and (most importantly) where the customer is."

Then the doctor continued with, "I have a packaging idea I would like to run past you." I leaned back in my chair and listened. "Once I sell this book to all the chiropractors, I can go through the manuscript with search & replace and change the word 'chiropractor' to 'dentist' and sell the same book to all the dentists. Next, I'll sell to all the medical doctors. Isn't that a great plan?"

"No," I said, "It sounds great, but it is a terrible idea. First off, it will not be all that easy to sell to your peers. It will take reviews in your magazines, displays at your conventions and lots of mail and telephone calls. Finally, word-of-mouth from one doctor will sell another. Do you really want to learn all about dentists? Do you want to read their magazines, join their associations and attend their conventions? You do not have time for that. But what you should do is publish this book. Then write the advanced book, then the business-forms book and then the little books chiropractors give to their patients. You want to become known as the publisher for the chiropractic industry."

Anyone who has ever been in sales will tell us that it is far easier to sell an additional product to an existing customer than it is to find a new customer. Stay in one field and keep adding products until you own it.

Over the years, I have written 117 books on 10 different subjects. I found that I could not keep up; I could not maintain an expertise in all of the fields. I could not even read all the free magazines I received. In desperation, to maintain credibility with my readers, I cut back to three categories: book writing/publishing, skydiving and expert witnessing-and it is still too much.

📖

The New "Book" Model

© Dan Poynter

Creating the Content ≡PDF ≡	Producing the "Work" ≡	Promoting the Editions

A. Set up.
Idea for your book
Quality project according to the Six Musts. WN-40
See *Writing Nonfiction: Turning Thought into Books*
Research the subject, title and competition.
Stores, Amazon, Ingram 615-213-6803
Get a model Book.
Draft back cover sales copy. Doc 116, WN Ch. 6.
Select a working title. *Writing Nonfiction*, Ch 5.
Set up the binder for the manuscript. WN Ch. 7&8
Assemble research materials into chapter piles.
 	
B. Build the content. WN, Ch 8.
1st draft. Assemble the elements
Write text in MS-*Word* in page-layout format.
Import digital photographs
Adobe *PhotoDeluxe* or *PhotoShop* or *PhotoSuite*
Import scanned drawings
Add art from Web
http://www.Clipbar.com
Find quotations on Web.
http://www.goodian.com/~garock/garock.html
Request stories from colleagues with email
Add URL hyperlinks to references
 	
2nd draft. Content edit. Fill in the blanks.
 	
3rd draft. Peer review for feedback. Use email.
Get testimonials for back cover, etc.
 	
4th draft. Copy edit (punctuation, grammar).
Fact check
Proofread
 	
C. Convert to: (*Writing Nonfiction*, pgs 29-30).
1. PDF file with Adobe *Acrobat*
2. LIT file, MS-Reader with RosettaMachine
 	
D. Get cover art
http://parapublishing.com/supplies.cfm?
	Publish: print & electronic versions. SPM Ch 11.
	
	A. pBooks (Photos & Dwgs: 300 dpi TIF)
	  1. Press (ink on paper)
	  2. PQN (short-run, disk to drum.)
	    Mass-Customization
	  3. POD (one at a time, disk to drum)
	    Need 300-500 to test the market.
	
	B. eBooks (72 dpi. Photos: JPG; dwgs: GIF). Interactive
	  Downloadable
	    From your site
	    From other sites
	  Portable eBook readers. PDF and LIT files.
	    Also in XML/OEB, Palm & MobiPocket
	  CDs & DVDs
	
	Media Asset Management
	Multi-purpose your core content.
	Wring maximum value out of your Work.
	
	A. Versions (downloadable) from your Web site
	  Audio version (Digital)
	  Special reports (spin off from book)
	  Articles (spin off from book)
	    Pricing pBooks & eBooks
	B. Sell from Web site (not downloadable)
	  Seminars/Speeches
	    Record and sell the audio
	  Consulting
	    Expert witness testimony
	  Compatible (non-information) products
	
	Help: http://parapublishing.com/supplier.cfm?
	Codes: WN: *Writing Nonfiction*; SPM: *The Self-Publishing Manual*
	For more information, contact
	DanPoynter@ParaPublishing.com; http://ParaPublishing.com
		Make your company "Website-centric".
		Set up pressroom.
		
		A. Book industry. Send sample books to:
		  Agents (if you wish to sell out)
		  Publishers (if you wish to sell out)
		  Distributor/bookstores/online bookstores
		  "Galleys" to pre pub reviewers-SPM Pg 176
		  http://parapublishing.com/getpage.cfm?file=/source/promote_reviews
		  Industry and early review copies. SPM Pg 179
		  Book clubs. See LMP & SPM, pg. 269
		  Foreign rights-translations. See ILMP & SPM
		
		B. Nontraditional markets. ID and Locate buyers.
		  Make Dealers (wholesale)
		  Specialty stores (think products not books).
		  Associations
		  Magazines
		  Events
		  Catalogs. SPM pg 297.
		  Premiums. SPM pg 262.
		  Fundraisers. SPM pg 265.
		  Military and government. SPM pg 262.
		
		C. Disintermediation: sell directly to individual
		  reader/buyers (retail).
		  Promote your book with:
		    Review copies to magazines. SPM-185
		    List: http://parapublishing.com/getpage.cfm?file=/bookroom.html
		    News releases to magazines. SPM pg 204.
		    Services
		      http://www.book-publicity.com
		    eMail announcements (broadcast email)
		    eZine: Newsletter/List
		    Business cards (no brochures)
		    Postcards (invite to Web site)
		    Online : email lists, chat rooms & news groups
		    Autographings/mini-seminars. See Doc 639
		      Posters & buttons
		    Radio and TV interviews. See Doc. 602

Chapter Four

Researching Your Topic and Checking for Competition

Before you begin your writing journey, you must do some research. You want to know how much information is available on the subject and if this book has been written before. Once you see what is out there, your approach, angle, hook, direction or niche may change.

Assessing the Market

If you decide to sell out by approaching an agent or a publisher, you will be asked for a proposal. The agent or publisher will want to know if other books have covered this subject lately. From this angle? How are books in this category selling? How large is the market? What is the median selling price of the books on this shelf? If you plan to publish yourself, you need the same information to make an informed decision.

What people are buying. Generally, women buy books on relationships, weight loss/exercise and spirituality. Men purchase books on business, organizational skills and sports related works.

Bookstores. Visit places where books are sold. Like libraries, bookstores vary in the types of books they carry. For example, books on business are plentiful in downtown stores, but there are few titles on the topic in the mall stores in the suburbs. Conversely, you are more likely to find a greater selection of parenting and relationship books in the malls than downtown. You will also find that the larger *superstores* have a much greater selection than smaller stores. Visit several stores, both chain and independent, to see the variety of offerings.

Stores carry only 40,000 to 80,000 of the 2.8 million books currently in print (available for sale). So the books you see on the shelves are the ones that are selling well. Make a list of all the books on your subject in each store. Note the title, subtitle, author, trim size, shape, type of cover (hard, soft), ISBN and price. Buy those you need for your research. While you are in the bookstore, also check the magazine rack.

Run your idea past the bookstore proprietor. This person usually knows what is selling and what the buying public is asking for.

Online bookstore databases such as http://www.amazon.com. List all the books that are available or in print as well as out-of-print books. Make a subject search and print out the results. Try several alternative words. For example, for a book on skydiving, try these words: skydive, skydiving, skydiver, parachute, parachuting, parachutist, freefall. Make a similar search for titles with the same keywords. Try several book databases.

Sort the books into publication-date order. See the brand-new books and go back 20 years. Notice what is being done and what has been done.

At Amazon, the readers evaluate the books. Record how many stars each title has. Amazon also reveals the sales rank of each book. Record how each book is selling against the others in its category.

After you do this, make a search on your proposed or *working title*. You'll learn more about titles in the next chapter. Don't worry when you read of other books that sound like the one you propose to write. Many books are poorly titled. But you must get all the books to check their coverage and to reference in your book.

Next, see how much information is available on your subject. You want to gather information on every book, magazine article, database and resource. Visit the web sites listed in the Appendix and use the search engines such as *Google, WebCrawler, Excite* and *Yahoo.* Check sites such as http://www.refdesk.com and http://www.tveyes.com. Type in keywords and the sites will collect articles and information for you.

This detective work can be great fun. One scrap of information will lead to another as you spend hours on the Internet, *the world's largest library.*

Call Ingram's automated stock and sales system at (615) 213-6803. Just punch in the International Standard Book Number (ISBN) found on the copyright page and back cover to check the rate of sale for the various books you have located. The automated voice will tell you how many books are stocked in each of the five Ingram warehouses, how many copies Ingram sold last year and how many they have sold so far this year. These numbers are not total sales figures, but since Ingram handles more than half of the books sold in the country, the figures give you an idea of the rate of sale and are good for comparison.

By now, you should be getting a good picture of what has been done, what has been done lately, the angles from which the subject has been approached, what is selling and the prices for which the books on that shelf are selling.

Now research all the magazines on your subject. See resources such as the *Standard Periodical Directory,* which lists information about thousands of magazines. See http://www.mediafinder.com.

Consult *Ulrich's International Periodical Directory* (listings for many U.S. and foreign periodicals). See http://www.ulrichsweb.com. Look at the newsletter directories such as Hudson's *Subscription Newsletter Directory.* PO Box 311, Rhinebeck, NY 12572. Tel: 914-876-2081, and Gale's *Newsletters in Print.* See http://www.gale.com.

Ask the reference librarian for the collection of *Publishers Weekly.* If you are researching a travel book, cookbook, directory, computer book or other common category, look for the special editions of *PW.* Periodically, the magazine devotes entire sections to specific genres. These sections will tell you what is happening with books in this field and will list most of the books about to be published.

Research the audience for your book by searching the directories of associations, magazines, stores and events. Will you be able to reach your intended customer?

Run your book idea past the librarian. These book professionals have a wealth of knowledge. Most will take an interest in your project and will suggest more references.

"We write to learn."
—**Bud Gardner, co-author, *Chicken Soup for the Writer's Soul***

How far back you must research your subject matter is up to you; you know your subject. For example, if you were researching parachutes, you would have to go all the way back to 1495 and Leonardo da Vinci. If you are researching computers, three months ought to do it.

Your bookshelves should have a number of books on your intended subject. Go through those books and photocopy the pages with information you want to include in your book.

Call or email authors and publishers of older, out-of-print books and ask how the book did. Most authors and publishers are helpful and will share this information. Since the book has run its course and is no longer available, you do not pose a threat to their business. They regard their books as members of the family, and most parents like to brag about their children. If the author or publisher has time, he or she will usually open up and tell you all about the successes and challenges the book had.

"They're there, they're mine, they're my children."
—**Norman Mailer, American writer
and Pulitzer Prize winner**

Ask people in your industry or association if such a book is needed and what you might charge for it. If they are dealers, ask how many they might sell in a year and so on.

> Before writing my first major book (590 pages, 2,000 illustrations, and 5,000 copies), I polled the parachute industry regarding its viability. Encouraged with the response, I borrowed $15,000 from my parents and had 5,000 copies printed.

Get a model book. Visit a bookstore. Check your book's section and then look into other shelves. Find a book you like-on any subject. Consider the binding, layout, feel, margins, typestyle, everything. Then buy it. Use this book for a model. Tell your typesetter (you may typeset it yourself) and printer you want your manuscript to look like this book. There is no need to create a new design when you can follow an existing one.

If you want your book to sell like a book, it has to look like a book. You will note that each genre (classification) in the store has its own special look. For example, books on business usually have a hard cover and a dust jacket. Books for professionals such as doctors, lawyers and accountants are hardcover without a dust jacket. Children's books are larger, four-color and have 32 pages. Cookbooks are wider than they are tall so they will open and lie flat. Travel books are lightweight and easy to carry.

Respect the category. Your book must look like the rest on its shelf or it will stand out as being "strange," and strange does not achieve a sufficient confidence level to sell. Do not break out of the mold on your first attempt. If your book is different, it will lose credibility. Potential buyers will think you are an amateur and not ready to be a serious author/publisher. In book design, different doesn't sell.

> Milt Strong writes and publishes books on square dancing. All his books measure about 41/2" x 8." He explains that dancers want a tall, skinny book so they can read the steps and then slip the book into a back pocket. He knows and caters to his customers.

Book printers will produce an acceptable book, but that book will be boring unless you provide some design direction. What usually happens is that the author/ publisher spends a great deal of time on the text and the manufacturing becomes an afterthought. The package design is left up to the printer. What we see today are 5 1/2" x 8 1/2" soft-cover books that look the same. Printers can supply foldout pages, gold foil on the cover, die-cut jackets, embossed covers and many other variations. All you have to do is ask. Get a model book so you can adapt an appropriate design and visualize your finished product.

Get all the specialized books on your subject. If you are writing a travel book, cookbook, life story, humor book, directory, computer book or a book about something in another common category, see the specialized books. These books will tell you how to write them, how to produce them and, most importantly, how to promote them. It is often less expensive to buy several books on writing, producing and promoting your genre than it is to make one mistake. Also, to help you throughout the process, pick up a copy of *The Self-Publishing Manual*. See http://Para Publishing.com.

Chapter Five

Your Book's Title and Subtitle

Creating your title and subtitle will be the single most important piece of copywriting you will do for your book. A great title will not sell a bad book, but a poor title will hide a good book from potential customers. Both your title and subtitle must sell your work. They are the hook that gets a potential buyer's attention.

Obviously the title sells this book because the pages are blank

"If I had titled my book *How to Defuse Conflicts* or even *Avoiding Verbal Combat*, how many publishers (and later customers) would have looked at it? *Tongue Fu!* got me a publisher, buying readers and later lots of media attention."
—Sam Horn, author and speaker

Select a *working title* now so that you can improve on it as you develop your book. Start with a short, catchy and descriptive title, and add a lengthy, explanatory subtitle.

"Choose a title for your book at least as carefully as you would select a given name for your firstborn child."
—Nat Bodian, author, *How to Choose a Winning Title*

Here are some best sellers or classics that underwent a title change prior to publication. The original titles are in parentheses.

- 📖 *All the President's Men* (At This Point in Time)
- 📖 *Everything You Always Wanted to Know About Sex but Were Afraid to Ask* (The Birds and the Bees)
- 📖 Valley of the Dolls (They Don't Build Statues to Businessmen)
- 📖 *Pride and Prejudice* (First Impressions)
- 📖 *Roots* (Before This Anger)

Comedian Mort Saul tells this story on the importance of titles: One method of bolstering sagging sales is to republish a book with a new, more provocative title and an eye-catching cover design. To illustrate, he told of a new paperback he had seen in a drugstore. On the cover was a dramatic picture of a Cossack sweeping a half-clad maiden onto his horse. In large red letters was the title: *This Is My Flesh*. And underneath, in small letters, was the statement, "Formerly published under the title *Introduction to Accounting*."

Keyword. The first word of the title should be the same as the subject whenever possible to make the book easy to find. The book will be listed in Bowker's *Books in Print* by title, author and subject. If the title and subject are the same, you have doubled your exposure. Most other directories list only title-in alphabetical order.

> I wrote the first book on the new aviation sport of hang gliding back in 1973. I called the book *Hang Gliding, the Basic Handbook of Skysurfing*. The new sport was called hang gliding on the West Coast and skysurfing on the East Coast. No one knew which name would ultimately take over. I covered myself by using both keywords in the title and subtitle. Years later, hang gliding won out over skysurfing and pilots were mounting motors on their gliders. I changed the title of the 10th edition to *Hang Gliding, The Basic Handbook of Motorized Flight*.

On the other hand, if you come up with a fantastic title and it does not begin with the keyword, it is possible that you may sell so many more copies of the book due to the title that the directory listings become unimportant.

Most book listings do not describe the contents, so your subtitle should explain clearly what the book is about. For example, *Computer Selection Guide; Choosing the Right Hardware & Software: Business-Professional-Personal* is listed under the heading "computers," while the rest of the title and subtitle clearly explain what the book is about.

> The title for *Is There a Book Inside You?* came before the book was written. Mindy Bingham came up with the title, and then she and I wrote a book around it. Based on just the title and cover art, the book club rights were sold to Writer's Digest. The text had not even been completed.

Review *Books in Print*, an online bookstore such as Amazon.com, a dictionary and a thesaurus when searching for a title.

If your title is not clear, potential buyers may not find your book because it has been mis-shelved. Or, they may not recognize it as being an important subject to them.

Seven Tips for Terrific Titles

1. Make your title specific, familiar and short. The title should be easy to remember and easy to say. The words should relate well to each other. Ollie North's book was titled *Under Fire*. Alan Dershowitz wrote *Chutzpah*. And

Derek Humphrey penned *Final Exit*. Keep your title short and snappy.

> "Your title should be five words or less or people have to use their brains to repeat it."
> **—Jeff Herman, literary agent**

Books in Print uses a 92-character computer field. Make sure your title and subtitle tell the whole story and do not go over 92 characters. Some of the industry electronic ordering systems limit the title to 30 characters. Books are ordered by ISBN; the 30-character title is just a reference.

2. Do not start your title with a number as in "1,001 ways to ...". These titles are hard to catalog and then hard to find. Catalogers have to decide: does the "1" go above the letters, under "one" or under "thousand"? What if just 10 percent of your potential buyers can't find your listing?

> "Authors, as a rule, are poor judges of titles and often go for the cute or clever rather than the practical."
> **—Nat Bodian, author, *How to Choose a Winning Title***

3. Think of the image being conveyed. The title should project a warm, successful, positive image. Consider, for example, a book titled *We, the Lonely People*. No one wants to admit he or she is lonely; no one wants to be seen reading this book on the bus. Bookstore browsers are even reluctant to be seen picking up *The I Got Dumped Handbook*.

The title must grab attention and make a promise. Think about other products that say *Buy this hair spray and you will get a date Saturday night*. Good book titles are the best teaser copy in an ad or on the shelf. Think of good teaser copy and try it for a title.

Which title would sell more books: *Five Days* or *Five Nights*? If you change just one word, the picture is completely different.

Books with prevention titles such as *Don't Get Burned* and *How to Avoid Bicycle Theft* are hard to sell. Try to make the title positive. Rather than *Don't Be a Victim*, how about *Fighting Back; Taking Charge in Assault, Rape and Carjacking*?

4. Make your title specific. This is the age of specialization. Today, each book and magazine is aimed at a tightly focused, highly targeted audience.

A test was made by running large ads for a book with two different titles. One was named *The Art of Courtship*, and the other was called *The Art of Kissing*. *The Art of Courtship* pulled 17,500 orders, while *The Art of Kissing* sold 60,500 because it was more specific. In another test, *Eating for Health* sold 36,000 copies, while *Care of Skin and Hair* sold 52,000 copies. And here are some more: *The Tallow Ball*— 15,000; *The French Prostitute's Sacrifice*—54,700. *The Art of Controversy*—very few; *How to Argue Logically*—30,000; this title includes a promise. *An Introduction to Einstein*— 15,000; *Einstein's Theory of Relativity Explained*—42,000; the new title is more specific and makes a promise.

Customers buy the specific over the general. Put your No. 1 benefit in the title and subtitle of your book and make the description specific.

5. Beware of working titles. Working titles are dangerous because they can become too familiar while being misleading or meaningless to potential customers.

> *Choices, a Teen Woman's Journal for Self-Awareness and Personal Planning* was a hot seller, but it could not be used in schools unless there was a version for the boys. So the authors wrote a new book. Working titles ranged from *Choices II* to *Choices Too*, and even *Son of Choices*. What sounded ridiculous in the beginning became familiar and sounded fairly good. Finally the three female authors settled on *Changes* but found that men did not like it. After discussions with a number of men, they agreed to title the book *Challenges, a Teen Man's Journal for Self-Awareness and Personal Planning*. Most men rise to challenges but do not like changes. Consider the potential customer.

6. Use generic, not proprietary names. Some titles may be part of a trademark. For example, *Checkerboard Square* belongs to Ralston Purina. Avoid trademark infringement problems by steering clear of proprietary names.

And speaking of legal issues, be aware that titles cannot be copyrighted. One reason is there are too many books and too few words in the language. Check *Books in Print* and *Forthcoming Books in Print* for competing titles. Search an online bookstore such as Amazon.com.

7. Don't be slavishly imitative. Make sure your title does not *sound* like the title of an existing book. Booksellers may palm off someone else's book on the customer who asks for yours.

Do not waste your efforts competing for attention with a book with the same title. Spend your time selling your book.

However, a play on words may aid recognition. People remember a well-turned phrase better than a dull word group. Dottie Walters wrote a book titled *Speak & Grow Rich*, playing on the famous Napoleon Hill book *Think & Grow Rich*. And, of course, we have seen *The Joy of* everything from cooking to safe sex.

Here are some more sound-alike titles: *Dancing with Lawyers* by Nicholas Carroll. And some relationship books by Bob Mandel: *Heart Over Heals*, *Two Hearts Are Better Than One* and *Open Heart Therapy*.

What is a good title? It is one that sells the book.

About Your Subtitle

While your title should be short, the subtitle ought to be longer and more illustrative.

"The title should be short enough to be quickly readable, but long enough to identify the book's subject, its level and its coverage. Sometimes-particularly with books oriented toward business and management-the book's prime benefit should be part of the title as well. Most such books have compound titles separated by a colon, with the main content up front and an explanation after the colon."
   —Nat Bodian, author, *How to Choose a Winning Title*.

An example of a very long and descriptive title and subtitle is *Parachuting I/E Course: A Program of Study to Prepare the Expert Parachutist for the USPA Instructor/ Examiner Written Examination*. Certainly this subtitle tells precisely what the book is about.

A subtitle may be used to distinguish one title from another. There are more than a dozen books titled *Getting Published*, but each has a unique subtitle.

Does It Work?

How do you know if your title works? Take it out on the road. And, see what your competition is doing.

Title testing. Make up a list of possible titles and subtitles and test them on your friends. Show them a title and ask, "What is the book about?" How do they react? Do they perk up? Remember that big corporations spend lots of money testing names for new products. Record reactions. But make sure they are being objective and not just agreeing with you. Test the titles on booksellers and librarians; they know the customers, books and the business.

Visit a bookstore. Look in that section where your title will be. Then look in other sections. Which titles catch your eye? Will your title stand out?

If you get stuck, move on to drafting your back-cover sales copy. That process can help you find a title/subtitle.

Your working title and subtitle will evolve as you write and your book unfolds. Drafting your book is part of the journey; you are on your way.

"There are book titles that deserve better books, and there are books that deserve better titles."

Chapter Six

Your Book's Covers

Draft your covers before you write your book. To focus on whom your customers are and what you plan to share with them, draft your back-cover sales copy first. Does that sound backward to you? Think about it: Everyone judges a book by its cover. Like it or not, no one reads the book before making a buying decision. Consumers only browse it in the store. Sales reps carry only book covers and jackets to show store buyers; wholesalers and distributors say, "Just send us the cover copy." All buying decisions are made on the illustration, design and the sales copy on the outside of the book. Yes, packaging is everything.

Each year, U.S. industry spends more than $50 billion on package design. Packages prompt buyers to reach for the product whether it is panty hose, corn flakes, hair spray or books.

"A book's cover is absolutely the single most important thing about the physical object that is a book."
—Betsy Groban, Little, Brown and Company, Inc.

Stores display tens of thousands of books with the spine-out. With all this congestion, it is hard to get attention.

"Books sell five times faster when displayed face-out."
—Michael Larsen, literary agent

The package outside sells the product inside. The bookstore browser spends just eight seconds on the front cover and 15 seconds on the back cover—assuming the spine was good enough to get him or her to pull it from the shelf.

Your book-cover designer will lay out the package, incorporate the illustration, put it all on a disk and send it to your printer, but you must draft the sales copy. The book cover work sheet in this chapter will take you step by step through the sales copy drafting process. Use your computer so you will be able to move the copy around easily once you have entered it.

Spine

In the store, your book will be displayed spine-out only. There just is not enough room on the shelves for face-out stocking. Initially, all the potential buyer will see is the spine.

Today, technology allows allow us to stack the characters on the spine, making the title easier to read. It is no longer necessary to make the bookstore browsers tilt their heads to one side. Use a bold, block sans serif typeface. Try Arial MT Black (bold).

**A vertically stacked spine with
block letters is more legible**

Keep the spine simple and uncluttered. Limit the information to the necessary: the title, the last name of the author and maybe a symbol to catch the eye. Print the title on the spine, but leave off the subtitle unless it is short and is needed to explain the book. If you can abbreviate the title, the fewer words will stand out even more.

My book *Word Processors and Information Processing, What They Are and How to Buy* has just the words Word Processors on the spine. These two words are enough to catch the eye of the browser.

Make the spine type as large and as bold as possible. Do not use reverses (white on a dark color) unless you use large block white letters on a very dark background. Do not use script, thin characters or any type style that is hard to read. Remember that you are very familiar with your title and would recognize it even if it were written backward, but your potential buying public has to be able to read the title easily.

Your Front Cover

The cover should stand out. It must be easy to read and uncluttered. The title should be the focus. The cover should make you want to pick up the book to see what it is all about. The cover will display the title, subtitle, author's name and a related illustration with impact. Think of the cover as a billboard.

Place the title near the top of the cover

Title and subtitle placement. Put the title near the top of the cover. The book may be displayed on a rack with only the top one-third peeking over the book in front of it. Do not print the title on a busy background (such as in a tree) or it will be hard to see. Place the title in a clear space or strip in a plain background.

"A book has got to be appealing and jump off the shelf."
**—Robert Erdmann, past president,
Publishers Marketing Association**

Use just the author's name. Do not add *by*. If there is a name on the cover, it *must* be the name of the author. Exceptions are when the author is an organization or when two or more people made significantly different contributions. For example, *Written by* and *Illustrated by* distinguish the author from the artist of a children's book.

Where there are two or more authors, they may be listed alphabetically or the one best known to potential buyers may be listed first.

> I write books on how to write and publish. Mindy Bingham writes children's stories and about teenage self-development. Poynter is listed before Bingham on the cover of *Is There a Book Inside You?* This way, the book can be found in directories listed with Poynter's other writing books rather than with Bingham's. Think sales, not ego trips.

Hype. Some books include a line of hype, but this addition will not be necessary if your title and subtitle tell the story. On smaller-format fiction mass-market paperbacks, the hype formula consists of 12 words of hype on the front cover and 75 on the back cover. They use words such as *stunning, dazzling, moving* and *tumultuous*.

Stickers. Sometimes we encounter new information after the books are printed. For example, the book may win an award. To add value to the book, you may have gold-foil stickers printed to hand-apply to the covers. If they are installed at an angle, they won't look like part of the printing and will seem more important.

Illustration. Use original art and match the art outside with the action inside.

For an action book like hang gliding, consider an action photograph. For non-action subjects, consider original art. Use four-color art; don't try to save money on printing.

Make your book recognizable to its intended reader. Here are some examples: *The Green Beret's Guide* has a camouflage background, *Trivia Crosswords* has a crossword puzzle design, *Advertising in the Yellow Pages* is yellow and *Easy Halloween Costumes for Children* is orange and black.

Use of a related background makes the subject of the book instantly recognizable

Certain types of books have specific design formulas. For example: science fiction will have an action illustration with a man, a monster and a helpless maiden. Science fiction covers look like movie posters. The cover on children's books usually displays an illustration from inside the book. Mass-market paperbacks have a lot of color and hype because they have to compete for attention with magazines on newsstands. Classics often depict a painting from a museum. Mail-order books need clear graphics and type that will show up well in small black-and-white photographs in brochures and ads.

"I know when I see a really attractive jacket that the publisher is behind the book (with promotion) and, of course, I pay attention to it.
—Leslie Hanscom, *Newsday*

Background color. Avoid black: It shows smudges, scratches and fingerprints.

Date. Avoid putting the date in the title or on the cover (2005 edition). When the year is half over, the books appear to be old. Selling a cover-dated book is like selling calendars: you never know how many to print. You usually have too many or too few at the end of the year; you rarely come out even.

For now, scan in some *trial* cover art, set the type and print it out. Then cut the front cover, spine and back cover apart and insert the pieces into your binder's clear outside pockets (more about the binder soon). Your book is taking shape.

Your Back Cover

The back cover is important sales space. Use it for your promotional message. Don't waste this prime territory. Remember that potential buyers will spend only 15 seconds here, assuming they get this far. You must hook them immediately and hold them or they will put the book back on the shelf. To be successful, back covers must make promises and stress compelling benefits to the potential buyer.

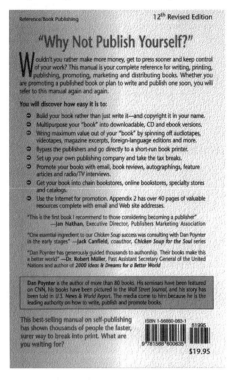

Back Cover of *The Self-Publishing Manual*

"Anyone who says you can't judge a book by its cover has never met the buyer from Barnes & Noble."

—Terri Lonier, *Working Solo*

Note that the author's picture is not on the back cover. If you have a recognizable face, use it to capture attention and sell the book. Otherwise, do not succumb to ego trips.

About the Author

Dan Poynter fell into publishing. He spent eight years researching a labor of love. Realizing that no publisher would be interested in a technical treatise on the parachute, he went directly to a printer. The orders poured in, and the author was suddenly a publisher.

In 1973, he became interested in a new aviation sport but couldn't find a book on the subject, so the skydiver and pilot sat down and wrote one. So far, *Hang Gliding* has sold over 130,000 copies—a best-seller!

Continuing to write, Dan has produced over 80 books and revisions, some of which have been translated into Spanish, Japanese, British English, Russian and German. His books are loaded with facts and figures and detailed inside information. They are always up to date because he revises them before going back to press.

Dan is an early adopter. He believes in buying machinery and has always been on the leading edge of technology. He published the first laser-typeset book in 1981. He was the first to send a galley to *Publishers Weekly* electronically in 1983. He embraced the fax in the mid-1980s and pioneered fax-on-demand to sell reports. He has been selling downloadable reports from his Web site since 1996.

Dan has always accurately predicted the future of publishing. Now the required technologies he describes have converged. Dan is about to open your eyes to the "New Book Publishing Model."

Dan was prompted to write this book because so many authors and publishers wanted to know his secret to selling so many books. Now he is revealing to you the secrets of writing, producing and promoting *your* book—the good life of self-publishing.

Remember the Front Matter

There is more room in the front matter to chronicle your exploits. Readers want to know what you look like and they know more about you than you know about them. We will discuss front matter, the material in the book before Chapter 1, later in this book.

See the back cover of this book as another layout example. Now here is an explanation of what goes on your back cover.

	Book Covers Work Sheet	2 pages—Document 116—page 1
(Back Cover)		(Front Cover)

Category:

Headline:

Sales copy/description. What is the book about?:

Promises & Benefits
You will discover:
-
-
-
-

Testimonials (names of endorsers):

1.

2.

3.

Why the author is qualified to write this book:

Closing copy:

Price: $ (ISBN and bar code)

(Spine)

T I T L E

of

B O O K

Title:

Subtitle:

Author's name:

Foreword by:

Back-cover work sheet

Category. Visit a bookstore and check the shelf where your book will be displayed. Note the shelving categories above the books. Listing the category\subcategory on the back cover of your book will ensure that your book will be easy to find—because the bookshop personnel will place it on the right shelf. You have the power to get your book on the shelf of your choice—if you list the category on the back cover.

Headline. Now you need an arresting headline addressed to potential buyers. You want them to relate to and identify with the book. Do not repeat the title here; do not bore the potential buyer. You have already said it on the front. Use an alternate approach. For example, *The Self-Publishing Manual's* headline is *Why Not Publish Yourself?*

Description. Concisely (in two to four sentences) state what the book is about. What will the reader gain by reading this book?

Bulleted promises or benefits. Promise to make readers better at what they do. Pledge health, wealth or a better life.

Focus on who your audience is and what that particular group wants.

You will discover how to:
- (benefit)
- (benefit)
- (benefit)
- (benefit)

Testimonials, forewords, endorsements and quotations or "blurbs" sell books because word of mouth is one of the most powerful forces in marketing. We will cover getting testimonials and forewords from influential people in the chapter on writing.

Author bio. Show that you are the ultimate authority on the subject. Just two or three sentences will do. You will write a whole page on yourself in the front matter of the book.

Closing copy. End with a sales closer in bold type. Ask the browser to buy the book. Use something like "This book has enabled thousands to _____ and it will show you the way too."

The bar code with International Standard Book Number (ISBN) comes at the end. The bar code on a book identifies the ISBN, which in turn identifies the publisher, title, author and edition (hardcover, etc.). Make room for, but do not worry about, the bar code and ISBN just now. The smaller code to the right of the big block is the price extension. When you need more detail, see Document 112 at http://parapub.com/getpage.cfm?file=products.html

**Mock up your cover and print it out
in color with an inkjet printer**

Price. Bookstores like a price on the book. Never locate the price at the top of the back cover; the price is a turnoff, so place it at the end of the sales copy. Remember: benefits at the top, features at the bottom. If this is a hard-cover book, place the price at the top corner of the front flap.

To arrive at a tentative price, visit a bookstore and check the shelf where your book will be. Find other books as close to your subject as possible. Would the buyer of these books be a potential customer for your book? Select a price in the middle. If your book is priced higher than the others, it will be priced out of the market. If it is priced lower, it will look cheap. Remember that your book's price will be compared with other books on its shelf.

Later, when you get printing bids, you will have to balance the production cost with your sales price. The cover price must be at least eight times the printing bill. So, if the production cost is $2 each, the cover price must be at least $16, but make it $15.95.

"The cover is your primary marketing tool."
—Dawson Church, publisher

Now your title, subtitle, back-cover headline and benefits may be swapped. Once you have them written down, you may wish to move some of them around. Perhaps one of your benefits would be a better subtitle.

There are people who make their living designing covers. They work with color and type. They know where to place the title and bar code. They not only lay out covers, they work with printers to make sure their design is carried out. Designers provide a great service and should be consulted. Cover Artists are listed at http://parapub.com/su pplier.cfm Check their web sites and see their styles. Find an artistic style to match the mood of your book.

"Always use trained professionals to produce your cover. A bad cover can cost you a hundred times the money you think you saved in the form of lost sales."
—Dawson Church, publisher

The mechanics. Covers today are created on a computer. Once your cover artist has the basic design, you may spend some time moving type, changing other graphic elements or altering colors. Just ask your cover artist to attach the cover image to an email message. Then view it on your monitor or print it out with a color inkjet printer. The colors will not match perfectly, but you will get a good idea of what your artist has created. Your artist can also send you a more accurate color *comp* to view via a delivery service. We find the ink-jet printout is close enough.

If you decide to forgo the print edition of your book and publish just the electronic version, you will still need a cover image to sell it.

Online bookstores such as Amazon.com want a flat, straight-on image of the cover. They do not want an angled shot that shows the thickness of the book. Flat images will also be used on your web site and will be provided to reviewers and dealers. You can create this type of image by scanning your finished cover.

Hardcover or soft? Traditionally, books were issued in hardcover with a dust jacket first. The early adopters bought this edition. A year or so later, the book was reissued in a soft-cover or perfect-bound edition. Most people bought this one. If the book was selling well, a couple of years later the book would be reissued again in the smaller mass-market paperback edition for sale in supermarkets and drugstores. The budget-conscious people bought this one. The conventional thinking is that one edition does not rob sales from another because each sells to a different group.

After 1980, there was a "paperback revolution." Today, most books are issued solely in softcover. Most smaller publishers today produce soft-cover books to keep costs down and achieve maximum distribution. But if your goal is to use your book as an introduction to your work, consider hardcover. Hardcover is still considered to be newer, fresher and more credible. Splitting the run between hardcovers and softcovers often costs more than putting hard covers on the entire run. So, choose one or the other.

Respect the category. Your book must look like the rest of the books on its shelf. If the others are hardcover, yours must be hardcover or it will not appear to fit in that section.

Cost. You may spend $1,500 or more for the concept, design, production and file for a traditionally printed front/spine/back cover.

On the other hand, if you plan just an electronic edition and require only a cover image, you may be able to do this yourself. If you are on a tight budget for this project, add the title, subtitle and author's name to an existing image. You may choose from a variety of color photos and drawings at http://www.ClipArt.com. ClipArt.com provides 2.6 million royalty-free images for an annual subscription of $149.95.

Original cover art may cost more than $1,500, but you are buying a complete cover design, not just an illustration. Many artists will draw a picture for $300 or $400, but what you want is a complete front cover, spine and back cover (mechanical) on disk, ready to go to the printer. A good cover artist will coordinate the job so that you do not have to get in the middle relaying messages you do not understand. If this still sounds like a lot of money, you should know that most mass-market (smaller size) paperback covers run $3,000 to $4,000. Good cover art will cost a little more than a bad wrapper, but it will make a world of difference to the sales of the book. Invest the money; you will be proud of your book and glad you did.

"The most common mistake made by publishers small and large is cutting corners on the cost of covers."
—Robert Erdmann, past president,
Publishers Marketing Association

Working with your cover artist. Do not shackle your graphic artist with details. Do not say, *I want yellow with a drawing of...* Just provide general direction. Show him or her a *model* book you like and say you want your cover to be classy or rustic or one that says mystery. Then let the artist give you his or her best.

A good cover artist will read through the text and then try to incorporate the feeling of the book into the cover art. It is all one package; the art outside should match the message inside.

Dust jacket. Hardcover books with dust jackets have a higher perceived value and can carry a higher price. Jackets usually have a synopsis of the book on the inside front flap and a biography and picture of the author on the inside back flap. The sales copy outline should still be used for the back cover.

Most back-cover copy is weak and uninspiring. The title is repeated and then is followed by several quotations and a bar code and that's it! Haphazard copy is the sign of a lazy (and maybe inexperienced) copywriter. This lack of effective competition on the shelf will give you the upper hand.

Years ago, we said, "Write your ad before you write your book." This was to help you focus on whom you were writing to and what you were going to give them. Then we realized the most important ad you will ever write is your back-cover copy. Now we say: "Write your cover copy before you write your book."

Packaging is marketing. Put your imagination into your title and your advertising money into your cover.

Chapter Seven

Getting Organized: Setting Up Your Binder

Set up your manuscript in a binder. Find a three-ring binder with pockets inside. Get a 2" (thick) model and add dividers corresponding to the chapters you have preliminarily selected.

Go to:

http://parapub.com/getpage.cfm?file=/speaking/forms_b ank.html and get the free Document *WN-Book Writing Layout Template*. It is a PDF file. Print it out, three-hole punch it and insert it into your binder. You are making progress already; the book is taking shape. Now all you have to do is fill in the blanks.

A binder with clear covers will allow you to insert the mock-ups of your book's front and back covers

Make your writing project portable and you will make use of otherwise wasted time. Carry it with you at all times and you will be able to take advantage of unexpected time: a few minutes after lunch, waiting in an office for an appointment and riding public transportation. Keep the project active in your mind.

Setting up the binder will provide encouragement. Soon you will have a partial manuscript; the book will be taking shape, and you will have something tangible to carry around. This will make you feel proud and give you the flexibility to write and rewrite and to improve your manuscript while away from home.

"Would that I could stand on a busy corner, hat in hand, and beg people to throw me all their wasted hours."
—Bernard Berenson, 1865-1959, American art critic

Write your name and address in the front of the binder with a note that this is a valuable manuscript and should be returned if found. You do not want to misplace and lose your future book.

Trim size. Try to use 51/2" x 81/2" and 81/2" x 11" as a final size for your book whenever possible. The best size for most books is 51/2" x 81/2," but you may have to go larger for workbooks and other books that must open and lie flat as well as for lengthy books. If you have just a few large charts, consider foldout pages.

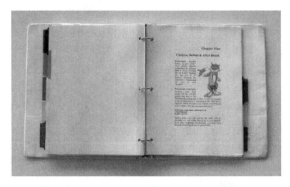

Use dividers and tabs to separate the chapters

Make your manuscript look like a page out of a book. Set your margins so that the text block will be about 4.2" wide and about 7" tall.

> Larsen/Proposal 1
>
> Part I
> Chapter One
> How to Get Paid to Write Your Book
> "If there is a book that you want to read and it hasn't
> been written yet, then you must write it."
> --Nobel-Prize-winning author Toni Morrison
> Want a million dollars to write a book?
> The subject? You can pick one later.
> Does this sound like a fantasy? It happened to Robert
> Woodward, coauthor of All's the President's Men. The catch is
> that it happened after his fourth book in a row hit the top of
> the best-seller list.
> Now is the most amazing time ever to be alive and a
> wonderful time for you to be a writer. You are blessed with more
> ways to make money from your ideas than ever. Writing your first
> book and making it successful can transform your life.
> Getting Paid to Write Your Book
> In The Insider's Guide to Getting Published, John Boswell
> notes that "today fully 90 percent of all nonfiction books sold
> to trade publishers are acquired on the basis of a proposal
> alone." If you can prove to a publisher that you can research,
> organize and write nonfiction with a rejection-proof proposal,
> you can get paid to write your book. But it will require a
> fundamental shift in your thinking from that of a writer with
> something to say to that of an author with something to sell.

Traditional manuscript—just words on paper

Traditionally, manuscripts consisted of double-spaced Courier type. Today, that format makes your Work look dated.

Trial-set your type. To save time and to be able to visualize each printed page, set your margins, header, page number, type styles, chapter numbers, chapter titles, first paragraphs, etc., before you write a single word. Then fill in the page.

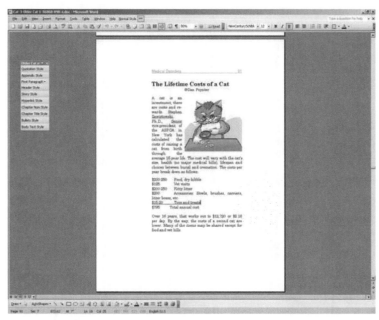

Set the margins, header and page number

To set your margins in Microsoft Word, click on *File\Page Setup* and change *top* to 1.8," *bottom* to 2.3," *left* to 2.5," *right* to 1.9" and *header* to 1.3."

To make a header, with the book title and page number at the top of the page, click on *View\Header and Footer.* Type in the tentative title for your book, then click on the *insert page number* icon that is in the header and footer box. Underline both your header and your page number. Then set them in *Arial* or *Tahoma*, 10-point type.

For your text, select a nice typeface such as *Book Antiqua* or *New Century Schoolbook* (sometimes called *Schoolbook* or *Century*). Click on *Format\Paragraph* and set the line spacing for *Single*.

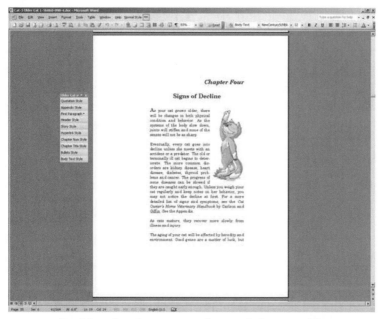

Position the chapter number and chapter title

When you write your book in book-layout format, you always know how many pages you have and you are trial-typesetting as you write. Now you are *building* your book; writing is just part of the assembly.

There are two pages to each sheet or leaf of paper. The *verso* pages are on the left-hand side and are even-numbered while the *recto* pages are on the right-hand side with odd numbers.

Parts of a Book

Most books are divided into three main parts: preliminary pages or *front matter,* the *text* and the *back matter.* We will discuss each of them in order. It is not necessary to have all the pages mentioned, but you do want to follow their order. Set up these sections as best you can, so the book will begin to take shape. You will make additions and revisions to the binder later.

Begin by placing dividers in the binder and insert a clean sheet of paper for each of the sections listed below that you wish to include. Fill in as much information as you have now. Use a pen to add to your manuscript in the binder as you progress. The collected information does not have to be neat or in order; the important thing is that now you have a place to store your material. As you add pages, as the binder fills up, you will have more work to carry as you venture away from home. When you find a few idle moments, open the binder and revise a page or two, bit by bit.

If you are itching to begin on your text, which is the heart of your book, you may wish to go to the next chapter at this time and return later to this discussion of front matter and back matter. But when we follow the New Book Model, some or all of the front and back matter pages will be desired. So, it makes sense to consider these sections as you are preparing your text.

Set up your binder in the order that follows and refer to this book for examples of each part. To understand how this book was assembled, see the Colophon in the Appendix.

Front Matter

The front matter is that material placed at the beginning of the book. It includes everything until the beginning of Chapter 1.

End papers may be plain or printed, are usually of heavier paper, and are glued to the inside front and back covers of hardbound (case-bound) books. End papers dress up the book and hold it together. End papers are usually not printed, but occasionally have appropriate maps.

Testimonials, endorsements and excerpts from reviews are being seen more and more on the initial pages of soft-cover books. This is important sales space.

The bastard title or half title is more often found in hardbound books than in paperbacks. It contains only the title and is a right-hand page. Until the later 1800s, books were usually sold without covers—so the buyer could have all his books bound in the same style for a matching library.

The bastard title page was just a wrapper for the text. It was often removed before binding.

The frontispiece is a photograph or *plate* usually found on a left-hand page facing the title page. Before modern printing machinery, illustrations were expensive to print, and the frontispiece might be the only picture in the book. Often the frontispiece was an engraving of the author. Today this page is commonly left blank or used to list other books by the same author.

The title page is on the right-hand side and lists the full title and subtitle of the book. This page may also include the name of the author or editor, the publisher, whether this is an original or revised edition, location of the publisher and the date.

The copyright page or *title page verso* is on the reverse of the title page and is the most critical page in the book. Proofread it a dozen times! Here you will print the copyright notice, show the printing history (number of printings and revisions), list the Library of Congress Catalog number, the ISBN, the Library of Congress Cataloging-in-Publication Data (CIP), name and address of the publisher and *printed in the United States of America* (to avoid export complications).

Your CIP data block may be obtained from the Library of Congress once you have published three books. Until then, contact Quality Books for this bibliographic information: http://www.quality-books.com/. A staff librarian will catalog your forthcoming title and will send you a data block ready to be pasted in to your copyright page. This bibliographic data can alternatively be drafted for you by a local librarian.

Those who know the book trade will often glance at the front and back cover and then turn to the copyright page. The copyright page is important in selling a book to the trade, so make it look professional. You want to appear to be a big-time publisher, not a kitchen-based word shop.

Each time you revise the book, it is worthwhile to change the copyright page in order to add, for example, *Second Printing, revised, 2005*, as this lets the potential purchaser know the book is up to date. Most big publishers do not make any changes to the copyright page and print a string of numbers on it instead. You will note: "10 9 8 7 6 5 4 3 2 1," which indicates to the trained eye that this is the first edition. Prior to reprinting it, the printer will opaque out the "1" on the photographic negative.

> William Crook, M.D., writes: In 1994, I went back to Random House and said, '*The Yeast Connection* needs revising. Much of the information is out of date." They replied, "We're not interested. It's one of our best backlist sellers." I went back to them in August of 1995 and asked them to work with me to revise the book. In October 1996, they informed me that they were going to reprint *The Yeast Connection*—unchanged. They felt it was their duty as a "responsible publisher." I objected. I sent a registered letter to the president of Random House. No response. They went ahead and reprinted the out-of-date book. It did not even include a warning about the danger of giving someone the common antihistamine, Seldane,(tm) along with fungal medication.

The dedication page. Some authors like to praise their family for supporting them during the book-writing journey. This right-hand page was used historically by writers to acknowledge their patrons, the people or institutions that supported them financially while they wrote.

The epigraph page contains a pertinent quotation that sets the tone of the book. Using a separate page for an epigraph is sometimes a nice touch but may be a waste of space.

The table of contents should start on the right-hand side. This page will include the chapter numbers, chapter titles and beginning page numbers. You can leave the page numbers out for now. Fill them in later when the book is formatted. Remember, when buying technical, professional or how-to books, some people turn immediately to the table of contents to check the book's coverage. Use some imagination when drafting your chapter titles—make them descriptive and inviting.

A list of illustrations is in order if the book is heavily illustrated, has many important tables or if it is a picture-type book. Most books do not need this list.

The foreword is positioned on the right-hand side and is a pitch for the book by someone other than the author. Try to get an expert in your field to contribute a foreword. It is very prestigious when a person with a recognizable name or a recognizable title is connected with your book. Contact one of the peer reviewers (described in the next chapter) about writing your foreword. Help this person by writing it yourself to demonstrate what you are seeking. Experts are busy people, and it is always easier for them to edit than to create.

It is doubtful that many people read the foreword, but they will notice who wrote it. The fact is most readers turn directly to the action. You may wish to note "Foreword by..." on the cover if that important name will help sell books.

If you include a foreword, note the correct spelling; it is not "forward." It is the "word" that comes before the text.

The preface is written by the author and tells why and how he or she wrote the book. It gets about as much attention from the reader as a foreword and appears on the right-hand side. If you have an important message and want to be sure the reader receives it, put the information in Chapter One.

Acknowledgments are a great sales tool. List everyone who helped you prepare your manuscript and book. People love to see their name in print, and each will become a disciple spreading the word about your great contribution to literature. On this blank sheet in your binder, add names of contributors as you encounter them so no one is left out.

The introduction defines the organization and limits of the work. The author writes it.

The list of abbreviations is only required in some very technical books.

The repeated bastard title is next, is optional and is a waste of space in most books.

Disclaimers are showing up in more and more books today. Lawsuits are an unfortunate fact of life in the United States, and while disclaimers are not absolute protection against them, the warning can't hurt.

Paraphrase the Disclaimer in this book and do not leave out the last sentence. Judges have ruled you must provide buyers with an alternative if they refuse to be bound by your disclaimer.

Obviously, if all the front matter pages listed above were included in your book, you would have a large number of pages already. You do not need all these pages, and it is recommended that you do away with most, except the title page, copyright page, table of contents, acknowledgments and the about the author and disclaimer pages. Check over several other books for layout, especially old hardbound books that followed convention.

Text

The text of the book is the meaty part on which the front matter and back matter hang. This is the second or main section.

Start your book off with an *action chapter*. It should be similar to the introductory part of a speech. Chapter One should arouse the reader and whet his or her appetite. Too many authors want to start from the *beginning* and describe their research or put a boring history chapter first. The reader wants to know "where to" and "how to." Do not sedate the reader in the first chapter.

It has been reported that most book buyers do not get past Page 18 in a new book. They buy it, bring it home, begin reading and then put it down on the bedside table. And they never get back to it. Your book has to be exciting in the initial pages to keep the reader involved and reading.

"It is the writer's fault, not the reader's, if the reader puts down the book."

—David Halberstam, author

Divisions with distinct but related sections sometimes are made in long books. The division title pages contain the name and number of the section and their reverse sides are usually blank.

Chapter titles should reveal the subject of the chapter to aid the reader in finding what he or she wants. The reader may be skimming the book in a store, pending possible purchase, or may be referring back to something he or she has read. In either case, you want the description to be as clear as possible. Chapter titles are usually repeated in headers at the top of the right-hand pages to help the reader find desired chapters.

The subhead is a secondary heading or title, usually set in less prominent type than the main heading, to divide the entries under a subject. Subheads can contribute a logical progression, aid in finding needed material and help to break up long chapters. Note the use of bolded subheads in this book.

Footnotes are not needed except in technical publications. If your book will be used as a research tool, readers may want the footnotes so they can follow up on the material. When footnotes must be used, some people recommend they be placed at the end of the chapter or in the Appendix. Placing extensive footnotes at the bottom of the page can make for some short pages and tedious reading.

Web site addresses can replace a lot of footnotes and make finding the references easier for the reader. Whenever you mention a company, product service or information source, add the Web address (URL). Include the longer address for the exact page rather than the opening page of the referenced site. The electronic versions of your book (downloadable, CD, etc) will hyperlink the web sites; the reader can click on the reference and go directly to the site.

Back Matter

The back matter is reference material, such as the glossary, resources and index, placed at the back of the book. It is less expensive to revise lists toward the end when reprinting; avoid printing addresses subject to change within the text section.

The afterword is sometimes seen in manuals. Often it is a personal message from the author to the reader, wishing the best of luck or requesting suggestions for improvement.

The appendix contains important lists and other resources; it may be composed of several sections. As you collect information on your subject, add resources to this section. Add other books, reports, associations, conferences, tapes, suppliers and so on. A book with a large appendix often becomes a valuable reference.

To save space, print just the company name and its URL. Area codes and other address info change too often. It is permissible to set this reference material in smaller type.

The glossary is an alphabetically arranged dictionary of terms peculiar to the subject of the book. Some authors like to save space and simplify use by combining the glossary and the index.

The bibliography lists the reference materials or sources used in writing the book.

The addendum has brief, subsequent additional data. It is printed as part of the book or on a loose sheet.

Errata are errors discovered after printing. The list is printed on a separate sheet and may be pasted in or loose.

Author's notes come next and include additional information in chapter order.

Be careful in your proofreading and you should not need addenda, errata or author's notes.

Colophon is Greek for *finishing touch*, and it details the production facts by listing the typestyle, designer, typesetter, printer, kind of paper, etc. The colophon is not as common as it once was but is still found today in special *labor of love*-type publications.

The index aids the reader in locating specific information in the pages and is particularly important in reference works. Many librarians will not purchase books without indexes, so plan on including an index. The index is at the very end of the book to make it easy to locate.

Assembling the index is not hard if you build it with your word processing program. Simply read through your typeset manuscript and list the keywords and the page numbers. List all the main headings, subheadings and words readers might look for. Double-post two-word listings ("ripcord housing" and "housing, ripcord"), and cross-reference different terms. Format the page in two columns, and set the type in ragged-right alignment. Then use your computer to *AutoSort* the list.

MS-*Word* has an automatic indexing feature, and there are professional indexers who can do it for you. See the American Society of Indexers http://www.asindexing.org.

The index must be revised every time the book is updated if the page numbers change.

Order blank. The last page of the book should contain an order blank; place it on a left-hand page—facing out. Check this book and see how easy the order blank is to locate.

Some readers will want to purchase a copy of your book for a friend, while others may want a copy for themselves after seeing your book at a friend's home or in the library. Offer your other books and tapes too. Make ordering easy for them by listing the full price including sales tax (if applicable) and shipping cost. Order blanks are easy and inexpensive—and they work.

Now your manuscript shell is built and you are ready to fill it in. You are on your way.

"As you grow older, you'll find the only things you regret are the things you didn't do."

—Zachary Scott, 1914-1965, Actor

Chapter Eight

Your Writing System

~

You have been working on your book, but you have not done any writing yet. That is the point. Many people sit down at the keyboard faced with a desk piled high with notes and with a head full of a lifetime of education and experience. They start typing and then grind to a slow halt. Some think they have discovered writer's block. It is not writer's block; they simply do not have a plan. They are not sure who their reader is or what they plan to deliver to that reader.

If you do the planning and research outlined in the previous chapters, you will have a road map that is easy to follow. When you sit down at the keyboard, you will not be able to type fast enough.

In the New Book Model, we no longer just *write* our book, we *build* our book. New technology combined with revolutionary changes in the book industry provides the author with the tools, ability and authority to design the entire project. Building books today is more like assembling a PowerPoint presentation than writing a manuscript.

Now, authors not only craft the words to convey their message, we insert photographs, drawings, hyperlinks and other enhancements as we build our book. We are continually thinking about helping our reader to understand and are adding visual aids as we write.

"Willie, why do you use a gun when robbing banks?"
"I find the best way to get my point across is to use a few well-chosen words and—visual aids."
—Willie Sutton, infamous bank robber

About Writers and Writing

Two important points before we begin writing. One is pen names (pseudonyms). Some wannabe authors spend far too much time dreaming up a *nom de plume* to write under. Unless you are writing racy romance novels, you should use your own name. When your book is famous, you will be glad that people know who you are.

Second, understand that there is a difference between being an *author* and being a *writer*. As an expert in your field, you have the potential to be an author. Whether you have the talent, training, inclination or time to write is not as important. Since you have the information to contribute to the project, you can always hire a writer to make your material interesting to read. Few politicians and movie stars have time to write, yet many of these celebrities are published authors. Most of them have contributed the information for their books through rough drafts, dictation or interviews, but few are responsible for their entire manuscript.

"Today's public figures can no longer write their own speeches or books, and there is some evidence that they can't read them either."
—Gore Vidal, American novelist and screenwriter

Lee Iacocca is the author or two best sellers, but he is not the writer; he employed two ghostwriters.

For more information on working with collaborators, see *Is There a Book Inside You?* by Dan Poynter and Mindy Bingham. http://ParaPublishing.com

Getting Started

There are many good writing systems if you are interested in writing your own book. The more mechanical-type approach described here is very effective for busy people. This system allows you to combine your book project with other activities so you can write while maintaining your busy schedule.

Break down the writing project into easy-to-attack chunks. Your book project may appear to be overwhelming, requiring more time and work than you can invest. So separate the project into parts. Think of these parts as eight or 10 or 12 speeches, or articles or term papers. If you can write 10 term papers, you can write a book.

The Pilot System

Pilot system. One approach to writing your book is to break it into parts using the *pilot system* of organization. Gather all your research materials such as magazine articles, parts of books, charts and photos from your own files, and anything you have written so far. Photocopy pieces from other publications. Cut the copies apart and place them in piles on the floor. Create one pile for each chapter. Review the piles. Move the pieces around. Add reminders to yourself.

"Sometimes I turn ink into magic. Other times I just murder trees."
—Randall Williams, Black Belt Press

It would be nice to employ the pilot system on an elevated surface such as a table or long counter, but in most homes, the elevated surfaces are already covered with important things. I make my piles on the carpet.

As you survey the piles on the floor, you will probably discover why we call this the "pilot (pile-it) system" of book organization.

Do not start writing at the beginning. The most difficult part of writing a nonfiction book is getting started, and the easiest mistake is starting with Chapter 1. Approached from Page 1, writing a book appears to be a long, steep, hard climb. That makes it hard to get started.

Nonfiction books have several parts—we call them "chapters." They are related, but all do not have to be in any particular order. There is not much *flow* to be concerned about. Start with the chapter that is the shortest, easiest or the most fun. You will probably draft the first chapter last—and that is OK. The first chapter is usually an introduction to the rest of the book, and how can you know where you are going until you have been there? So do not begin writing from chapter one.

The Four Stages of Your Book

A nonfiction book has four stages: the rough draft, content edit, peer review and copy edit. Later, we have typesetting, proofreading and printing. Each of these drafts may have several revisions. *Is There a Book Inside You?* went through eight second drafts.

"I rewrote the ending of *Farewell to Arms* 39 times before I was satisfied."
—Ernest Hemingway (1899-1961), American novelist

1. The first draft is the rough draft.
Just get your materials and ideas down on paper (and on disk).

"Writing is like making love. You have to practice to be good at it."
—Morris West, author, *The Clowns of God*

The written word is different from the spoken word. Without voice inflection, body language and pacing, we need to be clearer in our meaning. Remember, the reader can't ask for clarification. Contractions such as "she'll" are rarely used in writing except to provide emphasis. Use "she will."

Shorter is better. Use brief wording and paragraphs. Your reader wants the information; he or she is not reading your nonfiction book to be entertained.

"You become a good writer just as you become a good joiner: by planing down your sentences."

**—Anatole France (1844-1924),
French novelist and Nobel Laureate**

String out one chapter pile on your desk

"Think much, speak little and write less."
                                    —Italian proverb

To create the first (rough) draft of each chapter, take one pile and string it out on your desk in some semblance of order.

Look at the first couple of scraps of notes and digest them. Think about the person for whom you are writing. Remember the promises you made on your back-cover draft. Put the information into your own words and type as fast as you can.

Do not be concerned about punctuation, grammar or style at this point. There is no such thing as a publishable first draft. Just get your message into the computer and onto the hard disk. You will edit the text later. Since it is easier to edit than it is to create, the first draft is the hardest part, and we want to get through this more difficult creative process as fast as possible.

Copyright. Do not repeat any of the notes word for word. Much of the material is not yours, so copying could be plagiarism and you would be guilty of copyright infringement. Adapt the *ideas* from many sources so that your sequences of words are not *substantially similar* to any of them.

"The secret of good writing is to say an old thing in a new way or to say a new thing in an old way."
                    —Richard Harding Davis (1864-1916),
                            American writer and journalist

Copyright requires two specific acts:
1. Create the string of words. Come up with the idea.
2. Put them in "fixed" form; memorialize the words by writing or recording them.

If one person says something memorable and another person writes down the words, neither person can copyright the *sequence of* words. One person has to both create the sentences and put them in "fixed form."

Copyright covers a *sequence* of words; the author's presentation or *expression*. It does not protect *ideas*. If you read and blend the ideas of other authors and put the collective thought into your own words, that is perfectly legal. This is how most nonfiction books are written—from research.

Facts may not be copyrighted either; they are free for anyone to repeat or use in a manuscript. In *Feist Publications, Inc. v. Rural Telephone Service Company, Inc.*, 111 S.Ct. 1282, 1287-88 (1991), the U.S. Supreme Court held that the name and address listings (facts) in a telephone directory were not protected by copyright.

Borrow *ideas*, borrow *facts*, but do not steal a sequence of *words*.

Finding time to write. Morning people like to write early in the day when they are most efficient and the house is quiet. Evening people, however, are more productive after dark. Many writers like to set aside a few hours for their writing each day; they set a schedule and stick to it religiously. Others prefer to write in one long stretch.

> I like to barrel through on a 24-hour-per-day schedule. The clock gives way to chapters and I completely lose track of time. I turn off the telephone, give orders not to be disturbed and drink protein meals and coffee. This way, I do not have to take time out to eat. Every hour or so, I get up to go outside and run around my home. This marathon of writing and protein meals produces my books in just a few days and sometimes helps me lose weight at the same time. During these marathons, I do not read the newspaper or play the television in the background. I avoid all distractions and mentally concentrate on the project.

"I prefer marathon writing 10-12 hours a day until it's finished. People who write a few hours here and there will spend too much time reviewing their work to determine where they left off."
—Dianna Booher, author and speaker.

Don't like typing? Keyboarding is not necessary to get your thoughts and materials onto the hard disk. You can dictate that first draft with a voice-recognition program such as Dragon *Naturally Speaking* or IBM's *Via Voice*. It does not matter how you get those scraps of paper off the floor and the information into the binder.

"If you wait for inspiration, you're not a writer but a waiter."

Fill the binder. As you complete a few pages, a section or a chapter, spell-check it with your word processing program and put a printout into the binder. Then go on. Do not edit the material in the binder until you have completed the entire first draft and retired all your notes and scraps of paper. As the piles come off the floor, onto the desk and go from computer to binder, you will gain a great feeling of accomplishment. It is helpful to see progress as you write a book.

Carry your binder with you everywhere you go. Busy people often have trouble finding the time to return to their desk and "the book." With the binder system, the book is always with you. As you go through the day and find a minute here and there, open the binder and write in your changes, notes and comments. When you get a good idea, pencil it in. Whenever you lose momentum, enter your changes into the computer and print out new pages. This activity has a stimulating effect.

I was scheduled to speak in Santa Monica the day after the big '94 Northridge, California, earthquake. Not knowing which freeways were still accessible and what the traffic might be like, I left Santa Barbara three hours early for the two-hour drive. And I zipped right down Highway 1 through Malibu only to arrive at the hotel three hours early. Now, what to do with the time? I could not even go to the bar; I had a presentation to make. Fortunately, I was working on a new book and had brought my binder with me. I was able to sit in a quiet meeting room and get three hours of quality, uninterrupted work on this manuscript.

Ed Rigsbee called one day to thank me for the binder idea. It helped Ed a lot, but not for the reasons stated above. Ed had been working on the manuscript at his office, but I told him to carry the binder at all times. So he took it home. He called to say that once his wife saw the binder, she became much more supportive of the project. She even urged him to spend time on it while she did the dishes.

With the binder under your arm, the book will remain in your thoughts. Your manuscript will grow, and your book will improve. The binder concept is an anti-procrastination crutch and it works.

"I believe that 80 percent of writing is actually thinking."
—Tad Bartimus, author and journalist

With your binder in one place and your hard disk in another, you will not have to worry about the financial and emotional disaster of losing your work in a fire or other catastrophe. The binder is one of your backups.

Interior Art

Art for your book's inside pages can include photographs (halftones), line drawings, animated GIFs, backgrounds, cartoons, bullets, buttons, icons, horizontal rules and more. Just place them into the text as you write.

Line work is a clean black-on-white drawing without any shading or screens. If you have illustrations drawn to order, use the same artist for them all to provide consistency.

Halftones are made from photographs by breaking them up into tiny dots with a screen.

Much art is available to you copyright-free from http://www.ClipArt.com for a very low annual fee.

To find animations for your eBook, see http://www.AnimationFactory.com.

For custom-drawn cartoons, see http://www.cartoonresource.com.

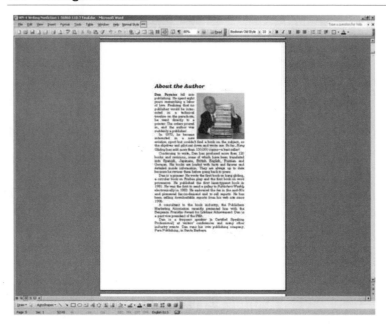

Scan or take photographs to explain your message

Photographs. Some of the most successful how-to books are those that manage to integrate words and pictures into an attractive teaching tool.

Scan existing photos, take new ones with a digital camera and/or import them from sites such as ClipArt.com. Load them into the computer, crop them, size them and put them in place. Decide whether you need a caption to make the image more understandable.

Use a digital camera, then import the JPG image into your manuscript. Use Adobe *Photoshop* or *Photoshop Elements* or MGI's *PhotoSuite* to convert them into black-and-white, 300 pixels per inch, .TIF files.

For online versions of your book, you will convert the images to 72 pixels per inch. Photos will be JPG and drawings will be GIF.

Images may be imported into the word processing file or "linked." If linked, you will find it easier to extract the photo for making adjustments, such as to the light/dark level.

You will note that as you add words, the image will move but it will always be anchored to the same place in the text.

Once you select a book printer, request scanning instructions so you can adjust the photos to reproduce well.

Photo release forms are advisable, particularly for pictures of minors. Permission might cost $20 to $500, but typically, your subjects are just happy to be in the book. A news photo does not require a release unless it is used in an advertisement. Permission fees are normally paid to the subject by the author upon publication. If you are concerned about the subjects in your photos, see the list of book attorney in Document 113 (free) at http://ParaPubli shing.com.

Sometimes you will overlook getting permission, and occasionally a subject will ask about his or her rights. The best way to handle this is to say that you are about to go back to press with a revised printing and, while it will cost you to replace the photo, you can take him or her out of the book. I have yet to hear of a subject who wanted to be deleted from a book.

Other photo sources. Some freelancers with a collection of photos will sell them for a few dollars each, or you can have photographs custom shot. Photo syndicates are in the business of selling stock photos. The chamber of commerce, private firms, trade associations and some governmental agencies have public relations departments that provide photos as part of their function. See their Web sites. Libraries and museums sometimes have photo files. When covering an event, contact the other photographers and get their cards. They may have just what you need. Picture sources are listed in *World Photography Sources*, *Writer's Market* and *Literary Market Place*. Ask for them at your library. Also see http://www.photosource.com/psb.

Video can be added to your eBook edition. In your electronic version, some of your images can move.

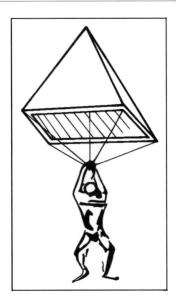

Drawings may be scanned, imported into the computer, cropped, sized and put in place. Decide whether you need a caption to make the image more understandable.

Copyright on images. Do not use art without permission. Do not copy photos from web sites or clip art from Microsoft Word. Take your own photographs and get copyright-free images from sites such as ClipArt.com. See http://www.ClipArt.com

Permissions for images. Typically, you may rent the use of charts, cartoons, comic strips, magazine articles and books excerpts. Just contact the Rights & Permissions Department of the publisher. A Dilbert comic strip may cost you $200, while an article from *Newsweek* might go for $100. The price often depends on your intended use. The publisher will charge you less for use in a report and more if you plan a film script around it.

Quotations. At this point you may wish to start gathering quotations. They may be sprinkled throughout your text or may be used at the bottom of the pages. Quotations are best used when they are placed to reinforce your nearby text.

Your advice will be more believable if confirmed by someone else.

If you want to quote another person, email him or her. Describe your project and ask if the quotation is still valid. Sometimes a person changes his or her mind about what was said due to intervening events. You want to the latest thoughts on the subject. It is also valuable to alert the person being quoted so that he or she can brag about being in your book.

Older quotations. There are many good quotation books, but it is even easier to find what you want online. Simply look for "quotations" with some of the search engines. One result will be http://www.quotationspage.com/search.php3.

Find older quotations at quotation Web sites

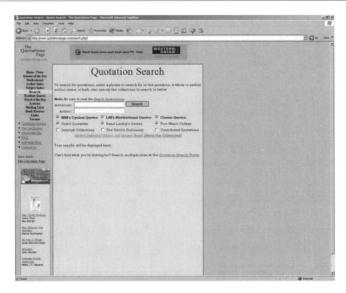

Find newer quotations at Amazon.com

Newer quotations may be found at Amazon.com. Many newer books have the *Search Inside This Book* feature. Just type in a keyword and each instance of it will come to the screen.

Encyclopedia Web site

Add to the quotations. Look up the people being quoted at an encyclopedia web site to find his or her date of birth, date of death if they have died, and a few words to describe what they have done.

By the way, the word is "quotation," not "quote," which refers to a price or the cost of a service.

Just another cliché. Occasionally inserting a familiar saying may help your reader to remember a point. A clich is something that lots of people say, and it conveys some sort of idea or message. In other words, a clich is a metaphor characterized by its overuse. See http://www.westegg.co m/cliche.

Stories make your points memorable. Solicit them from your colleagues. Set the stories in a different typeface or indent them to make the stories easier to find.

Clean up the submissions; add the name and URL (most people want to drive traffic to their web site) and email the piece back to the contributor for approval.

Hyperlinks. As you write, research the Web for URLs that will provide more information to your readers. Include these addresses in your text. The downloadable edition of your book will be even more valuable with these hyperlinks. As you visit these web sites, you will also pick up some late information, facts and figures that will improve your text.

Another enhancement to your eBook is hyperlinking words in the glossary to references in the text.

The first draft is the hardest part of writing a book. Now you can get to the fun: filling in the empty spaces.

2. The second draft is the *content* edit.
You have all your research notes compiled in the binder. You have quantified the project and can see where the holes are. Now is the time to do more research: Get on the Web (the world's largest library), call resource people and so on. Search for more information, get facts and background from encyclopedias, find illustrations, locate quotations and flesh out the text. It is time to fill in the blanks.

3. The third draft is the *peer review*.

Smart nonfiction authors take each chapter of their nearly complete manuscript and send it off to at least four experts on that particular chapter's subject. They enclose a cover letter like the one pictured.

Dear Steve,

You are an expert in this subject, and I value your opinion. Please comment on the enclosed chapter from the book I am working on.

Please make your changes, additions and comments with a red pen. You may comment on anything, even punctuation, grammar and style, but what I really need are comments on content. I want to be sure I have not left anything out and have not said anything that is wrong. Be brutal; I can take it. I would not ask for your input if I did not want it and need it.

If you will take part, I will mention your contribution in the Acknowledgments and will send you a free copy of the book as soon as it comes off the press.

I've enclosed the front matter and a mock-up of the front and back cover. Since "everyone judges a book by its cover," this will give you an idea of what the book is about.

As I am moving fast on this project, a self-addressed, stamped envelope is included for your convenience. Please get your comments back to me as soon as you can. Many thanks in advance for your help.

Sincerely,

Letter soliciting peer review

Shoot as high in your association or industry as possible. You do not have to know the peer reviewer personally. Just match your chapter to that expert's personal interest. As you research your subject, you will find who the movers and shakers are. They will be your peer reviewers.

You do not have to pay them for their contributions. Each peer reviewer is vitally interested in each particular chapter, so reviewing it is a privilege, not a burden. Just put their names in the Acknowledgements and send them an autographed copy of the finished book.

> Ken Blanchard, co-author of The One-Minute Manager Library, says, "I don't write my books; my friends write them for me." He explains that he jots down some ideas and sends them off to friends for comment. They send back lots of good ideas that he puts into his manuscript. Ken is being very generous, of course, and what he is describing is "peer review."

Use email or Priority Mail for both the sending and receiving envelopes.

If your book has 10 chapters, you will send out up to 40 peer-review packets. Some experts might get two or three chapters, but most will get only one. Do not overwhelm them. If you send the whole manuscript, most experts will put it on their desk with the best of intentions and never get back to it.

What you get back from your peer reviewers is priceless: They add two more items to your list; they delete whole paragraphs where the practice has changed; they cross out that part you thought was cute but was really embarrassingly stupid, and they sometimes even correct punctuation, grammar and style.

When your book comes out, you don't have to wait for adverse readers' reactions because you know the book is bulletproof. After all, it has been reviewed and accepted by the best.

You want these opinion molders to be excited and to tell everyone about your book—and how they helped you with it.

"There is no such thing as a publishable first draft."
 —William Targ, bookseller, collector, editor and publisher

Do not skip peer review. As much as 10 percent of your manuscript's content may come from your new friends and supporters.

Testimonials, forewords, endorsements and quotations or "blurbs" sell books because word-of-mouth is one of the most powerful forces in marketing. Anything *you* say about your book is self-serving, but words from *another* person are not. In fact, when readers see the quotation marks, it shifts their attitude and they become more receptive.

See the back cover and initial pages of this book for examples of testimonial usage.

> Harvey Mackay printed 44 testimonials in *Swim With the Sharks;* he had endorsements from everyone from Billy Graham to Robert Redford. Did these luminaries buy the book and write unsolicited testimonials? Of course not. Mackay asked for the words of praise.

Your mission is to get the highest-placed, most influential opinion molders talking about your book. You have more control than you think over the quotations you get, and testimonials are not difficult to secure if you follow a plan.

"Politicians respond at an astonishing 90 percent rate; otherwise, how would they get re-elected?"
—Kathleen Kain, author

Dream up three different endorsements from people that you would *like* to get a quotation from. If "This book changed my battlefield strategy. —Colin Powell" would look good, try it for now. You will attempt to get the quotation later.

The blurb should tie the endorser's background to the book. For example:

"*The Self-Publishing Manual* is the first book I recommend to new publishers."
—Jan Nathan, executive director, Publishers Marketing Association

Use *names* or *titles* recognizable in your field, sources who might influence potential buyers. Keep the blurbs to less than two sentences. There is little room on the back cover.

The easiest and fastest method of obtaining testimonials is a two-step process.

Step 1. Send each chapter of your manuscript out for peer review as outlined above.

Step 2. Approach your peer reviewers for a testimonial, now that you have softened them up. You are not surprising them by asking for a blurb for a work they haven't even seen.

February 30, 2005

Walters International
Dottie Walters
Post Office Box 1120
Glendora, CA 91740-1120   Testimonial

Dear Dottie,

I want to make you even more famous by including your prestigious name in my new book with a testimonial on page one or the back cover.

I know you are busy, and I recognize that drafting an endorsement is a hard work—requiring deep thought for most. So I have come up with a suggested line: one that ties in your background to my project. Note that it is short with a single message. Of course, you may edit this copy, change the reference to you or even start over (you are far more creative than I). You may even break my heart and blow your chance at immortality by round-filing this request.

If you elect to take part, please make any changes on the enclosed and return it in the self-addressed, stamped envelope.

I am enclosing a mock-up of the covers along with a Table of Contents to give you an idea of the concept. Of course, I will send you a complete manuscript if you want to see it. And you will get a copy of the book as soon as it comes off the press. But please respond soon. I am (always) in a hurry.

With best regards,

▰▰▰
PARA PUBLISHING

Dan Poynter
Publisher
DFP/ms

Testimonial Request Letter

Draft the (suggested) testimonial yourself. To get what you need, draft each (suggested) testimonial. Send it with a letter like the above.

Testimonial for

Writing Nonfiction
Turning Thoughts into Books

❐ I like this one:

There are many ways to be rich: having a family, doing good, being recognized and even earning money. Writing books and speaking professionally are two of the best ways to get there.

—Dottie Walters, Co-author ,
Speak and Grow Rich

❐ I can do better than that:

Signed:_____
             Dottie Walters

Please return to

Para Publishing
Dan Poynter
Post Office Box 8206
Santa Barbara, CA 93118-8206

Enclosed reply form

You will need endorsements on particular points, and you will need a variety. You certainly do not want all the blurbs to say the same thing, such as, "It is a great book." List your book's attributes and then draft some testimonials to match each one. Editing is much easier than creating, and most celebrities will accept the prompting readily.

Shoot high. Solicit testimonials from the highest-placed, most influential opinion molders in your association or industry. If you get turned down, come down a notch. Use the peer review technique, have faith in your work and give them a shot. It is easier than you think. Nothing ventured, nothing gained. See the list of celebrity directories in the Appendix.

Use blurbs everywhere. Gather a bunch and use the best ones for each particular purpose. You will need three for the back cover of your book. A hot one could go on the front cover. Extra blurbs are often put on the first pages of the book, in front of the title page.

Many news releases start with a blurb above the headline. The purpose is to get the attention of the editor so he or she will read the rest of the news release rather than toss it out.

A testimonial can be used as a teaser on an envelope of a direct mail piece. Save up your blurbs and use them where the endorser or title of the person will be recognized by the potential reader. Consult your bank of blurbs whenever you are writing promotional copy for your book.

Forewords are approached in the same manner as other endorsements. Write it yourself. What you get back from the writer is just longer than when you are gathering blurbs.

4. The fourth draft is the copy edit.
Now the manuscript is complete and we *are* concerned with punctuation, grammar and style. Get a wordsmith, a grammarian, a picky English pro. Some of these specialists call themselves "Book Doctors." Professional book editors pride themselves with being able to take a manuscript in any condition and make it right—which may mean completely rewriting it. Look for editors in the *Yellow Pages*, *Literary Market Place,* and http://parapublishing.com/suppl ier.cfm?

"I cannot think of anybody who doesn't need an editor, even though some people claim they don't."
—Tony Morris, editor and novelist

Submit your completed manuscript to your editor on a Zip disk, rewritable CD or simply attach the file to email. Have the editor make changes to the file and return it to you. If the corrections are made to a printout, you will have to enter the changes and then proof the changes. This will take longer and there are too many opportunities for error.

Final fact-checking. While the book is being copy edited, recheck all your facts, addresses and numbers. Our technology is evolving rapidly. Our society is changing quickly. And both are accelerating ever faster; everything is changing—rapidly. More than 24 percent of our population moves each year, and it seems as if area codes are changing daily. Do not just copy addresses out of other books. Call or check web sites to make sure they are still correct. Recheck all referenced URLS by clicking on them; make sure they are still valid and unbroken.

Editors usually can check facts faster than authors as they are less likely to get tied up in lengthy calls. You may wish to hire someone else to verify addresses.

To verify stories, email or fax the entire section or a page or two so the recipient will understand the context.

"Don't write so that you can be understood, write so that you can't be misunderstood."
—**William H. Taft (1857-1930), U.S. president and chief justice**

You are finished when the manuscript is 95 percent complete as long as it is 100 percent accurate. Waiting for one more photograph or one more item of information may border on procrastination. It is time to give birth. You have an audience that needs your information, the future of your company depends on getting into print.

Hopefully, you will sell out quickly, update the book and go back to press. And you will still be only 95 percent complete because our society, science and industries are evolving so rapidly.

**Your book is always a
work in progress**

Your book is never finished. Parts of it become out-of-date the moment ink strikes the paper. Note these newfound changes in a "correction copy" and keep it on your shelf so you will be ready to include the updates when the stock runs low. This is a growing work.

Book length. Your book should be between 144 and 288 pages. If it is too slim, it will not command the price you want to get. If, for example, your finished book is just 96 pages, add some resources. Do not "pad" the book, but add valuable listings of other books, audios, courses, etc. Both libraries and individual purchasers are more likely to buy books with lots of resources. Note the lengthy Appendix in this book. Other ways to lengthen the book—while making it more valuable and more interesting—are by adding quotations, stories and illustrations and/or to lay out the pages with more white space.

Your book should not be so long as to be intimidating and expensive. Paper is the most costly part of a book. An 800-page book will cost so much to produce that the price will be too high and few people will buy it.

> When I published my encyclopedic treatise on the parachute (590 pages and 2,000 illustrations) in 1972, a friend looked it over and said: "It looks kind of big. I think I'll just wait for the movie."

The ideal length might be 144 pages because books printed on a web press are assembled in signatures of 48 pages each (so 144 amounts to three signatures of 48 pages). Do not worry about page count now. When the manuscript is finished and about to be typeset, aim for multiples of 48 or at least multiples of 24.

If you are printing just a few copies using short-run digital printing, do not worry about signatures. These machines print both sides of single sheets; in effect, the signature is but two pages long.

Get help. Every smart author gets help. Seek peer reviewers, editors and proofreaders.

> I used to do everything by myself. I did the writing, content editing, copy editing, typesetting, proofreading, order taking, invoicing, shipping and even the floor sweeping. For many years, I was billed as the world's largest one-person publishing company. Today, I employ professional editors, proofreaders, typesetters, cover artists and office staff—not because I am lazy but because these people help me to produce a better book product.

Manuscript evaluation. If you have come this far and still do not have the confidence to proceed, contact author-publisher Gordon Burgett. He will read your manuscript and make recommendations for readability and will evaluate the book for salability. Gordon is an author who knows publishing from the inside. Contact him at Tel: 805-937-8711 or email: Gordon@sops.com

Typesetting. You have three choices. You may leave the book in *MS-Word*, You can pour the file into a page-layout program such as PageMaker, InDesign, Ventura Publisher or QuarkXPress or you may deal with a book designer/typesetter who is skilled at using page-layout programs.

To farm out the typesetting, contact a book designer, book typesetter, book producer or book packager. They all know what books look like and know how to produce them. See http://parapublishing.com/supplier.cfm.

Proofreading. Get a professional editor or proofreader to proof your final typeset copy. You want to avoid rewrites now, if possible. Basically, at this stage, you are only looking for typesetting and layout errors.

"If life had a second edition, how I would correct the proofs?"
—John Clare (1793-1864), English poet

To communicate corrections clearly, everyone working on the book must use standardized notations. See the table under *Proofreader's Marks* in your dictionary or go to http://webster.commnet.edu/writing/symbols.htm.

Convert the file to PDF. You can convert the *MS-Word* or page layout file to an Adobe *Acrobat* PDF, which in effect, it "photographs" the page you see on your screen. Acrobat integrates with Microsoft Office (including Microsoft *Word*). When installed, Acrobat automatically becomes an option in your Printer Dialog Box (File\Print: Printer Name). PDF has become easy to use and predictable—it saves time and money. An eBook version of your book will have excellent photos and drawings and they can even be in color.

Once in PDF format, your manuscript can be used in many ways or multipurposed. The four choices during conversion are:

📖 Print: Laser (toner) printer
📖 Press: Offset (ink) printing
📖 eBook: eBook for PDAs
📖 Screen: Computers and web sites

The PDF file is also much smaller than your word processing file, so it can be quickly sent as an email attachment.

You may purchase, rent or even try Acrobat free. See http://www.adobe.com/products/acrobat/main.html.

"Anyone who has ever taken a shower has had a good idea. The people who make a difference are those who get out of the shower and head for the keyboard."

Printing. Decide on your print run. If you want 500 to 1,500 books, send Requests For Quotations to digital printers. If you need more because of a prepublication sale, send the RFQs to offset printers. For a list of book printers, see the Appendix in this book. For instructions on drafting your RFQ, see *The Self-Publishing Manual*. http://ParaPublishing.com Do not worry about printing now, work on the writing.

📖

"Whether for information, argument or entertainment, the book is considered a repository. One expects the contents of a book to be available beyond the immediate moment—for days or years or generations into the future."

—Leonard Shatzkin, *In Cold Type*

Chapter Nine

Finding a Publisher
Finding an Agent

W e have all heard of the author who was rejected by 34 publishers before being "discovered." He or she was turned down after sending off the manuscript, unsolicited. Some of the larger publishers get more than 200 unrequested manuscripts "over the transom" every day. Most publishers rubber-stamp them "Return to Sender." It would be too expensive to open the packages and place the manuscripts into their return envelopes. These authors are being *rejected* without being *read*.

"A good many young writers make the mistake of enclosing a stamped, self-addressed envelope, big enough for the manuscript to come back in. This is too much of a temptation to the editor."
—Ring Lardner (1885-1933), American humorist and writer

How to find (the right) publisher

Better publishers specialize in one or two niche markets. They know their subjects and do not have to send your manuscript to a reader for evaluation. They also know how to reach the potential buyer and can jump-start your sales by plugging your book into their existing distribution system, selling to specialty shops and non-book dealers.

"The odds against an unknown writer getting a manuscript published by simply sending it directly to a publishing house are astronomical."
—Edwin McDowell, publishing correspondent,
The New York Times

The secret to finding the right publisher is simple yet very few writers do it: match your manuscript to the publisher.

"Authors do detailed research on the subject matter but seldom do any on which publishing house is appropriate for their work."
—**Walter W. Powell,** *Getting into Print*

To find these specialized publishers, check your own bookshelf, make a search at Amazon.com and visit a couple of larger bookstores. Look for books similar to yours. Match potential buyers: Would the buyer of this book be interested in your book? Look inside the books for the publisher's contact information. Addresses can also often be found at

http://www.BowkerLink.com
http://www.lights.com/publisher
http://www.pma-online.org
http://www.publishers.org
http://www.Google.com

When you call a specialized publisher, you will often get through to the top person. He or she loves the subject, wants to talk to you, knows what you are writing about and can tell instantly if the proposed book fits into the company's publishing plan.

To contact the right person at a larger publishing company, you will have to get by the *Call Prevention Department*; you are unlikely to get through without a name. See the listings of appropriate acquisition editors in *Literary Market Place*. Check the Acknowledgments in similar books; authors often reference their editor. Or, locate the authors of the other similar-subject books and ask for their editors' names and direct telephone numbers.

"Few of the major trade publishers will take a chance on a manuscript from someone whose name is not known."
—**Walter W. Powell,** *Getting Into Print*

Call the editor (or the publisher in a smaller house), refer to a similar title published and ask if he or she would like to see your manuscript. Then you will have someone to whom you can send your work. Do not take "no" for an answer. If you are turned down, ask for a referral. These editors know other editors who specialize in their field. Call the second editor using the first as a reference.

"It's harder for a new writer to get an agent than a publisher."
—Roger Straus, president, Farrar, Straus & Giroux

How to find (the right) agent

Many (larger) publishers prefer to have manuscripts filtered through agents.

"Eighty percent of the books published by major houses come through agents."
—Michael Larsen, literary agent

Some literary agents have a passion and a track record for certain kinds of books: cooking, travel, children's, business, parenting and so on. In this case, you must match your manuscript to the agents because they specialize too. Do not approach just any agent; do your homework. Find out what types of manuscript they handle. You want an advocate not a gatekeeper.

At writer's conferences, try this non-threatening way of approaching agents: Do not ask an agent to read your manuscript. Instead, say, "You are an agent and know most of the other agents. I realize agents have a track record in certain types of work. Which agents would you recommend for this manuscript?" You will be astonished at the positive reaction you get.

"Not all agents are created equal. Your goal is to find that special one who can support and sell your work."
—John Morgan Wilson, journalist and author

See the various agent directories such as *Writer's Market* or *Jeff Herman's Guide to Book Publishers, Editors and Literary Agents* or *Literary Market Place*. Numerous web sites offer information about agents. You can get a list of agents from the Association of Authors' Representatives by logging on to http://www.aar-online.org/. AAR members are not allowed to charge reading fees.

"Agents would have more time to read manuscripts if they spent less time doing lunch."

Another way to reach agents and publishers is the Maui Writers Conference Manuscript Marketplace; get information about your work into the hands of agents and editors for a fee. For registration forms, see http://www.mauiwrit ers.com/mwc_manuscript.html

Remember, above all else, *match* your book to the agent &/or publisher.

Many authors opt to make more money, get to press sooner and to keep control of their work. They self-publish.

📖

"Remember, all of this is negotiable. The contract looks like it is set in stone when you review it, but anything can be scratched out or inked in. If you want more books, a better discount, more help with marketing, negotiate for it. You may not get it, but you'll never know if you don't ask."

—Joe *Mr. Fire* Vitale

Afterword

As a writer and a publisher, I know that books reach more people than speeches, audios or seminars. I am sure you have a valuable message. I believe you should give the world a piece of your mind by putting your message in a book to expand your audience.

I do not want you to end here thinking, "That book was a fun read" or saying, "Dan must be a real savvy guy." I want you to resolve to get started on your book right now.

Researching and writing your book will be one of the most important things you ever do.

My system works. Thousands of successful authors have preceded you, and each week 15 to 20 authors send me copies of their finished book.

Dan Poynter

I am waiting for your book.

"The future belongs to those who believe in the beauty of their dreams."
  —**Eleanor Roosevelt (1884-1962), first lady, social activist, author, lecturer and U.S. representative to the United Nations**

"Give more to the world than you take from her. Write that book.
—**Dan Poynter, <u>http://ParaPub.com</u>**

Appendix

Resources

Now you can find even more specific information on writing and publishing. If, for example, you are writing a cookbook, get all the books on how to write, produce, publish and sell cookbooks. To avoid re-inventing the wheel, learn from the experience of others.

To be successful, you must have the best tools and the best resources. We have placed the specialized writing and publishing books into groups. Explanations, where they occur, are brief since it is assumed you will collect all the how-tos in your area of interest. Most books have resource sections and ideas that will lead you to even more information.

It is less expensive to buy these books than to make a single mistake.

The least expensive place to find dictionaries, style manuals and other reference books is in used bookstores. Some of the other books listed may be out of print. Search for them through a used bookstore or an online bookstore.

Writing Nonfiction Books

Is There a Book Inside You? Writing Alone or with a Collaborator by Dan Poynter and Mindy Bingham. $14.95. http://ParaPub lishing.com.

Writing the Nonfiction Book by Eva Shaw. http://www.eva shaw.com/

How to Write & Sell Your First Nonfiction Book by Oscar Collier and Frances Leighton. $9.95. St. Martin's Press.

How to Write a Book in 53 Days: The Elements of Speed Writing Necessity and Benefits Too by Don Paul. $14.95. Path Finder Publications.

Writing Nonfiction: Turning Thoughts into Books by Dan Poynter. $14.95. See http://www.ParaPublishing.com.

The Silver Pen: Starting a Profitable Writing Business from a Lifetime of Experience by Alan Canton. http://www.adams-blake.com

Autobiographies, Memoirs, Life Stories

The Times of Our Lives, A Guide to Writing Autobiography and Memoir by Mary Jane Moffat. $8.95. John Daniel and Company, http://www.danielpublishing.com/

How to Write the Story of Your Life by Frank P. Thomas. Unique approach to memoir writing. Resources. $12.99. Betterway Books.

How to Write Your Autobiography by Patricia Ann Case. Unique autobiographical outline. $7.95. Woodbridge Press, http://www.woodbridgepress.com.

How to Write Your Own Life Story: The Classic Guide for the Nonprofessional Writer by Lois Daniel. A guide with personal experiences told in the first person. $12.95. Chicago Review Press, http://www.ipgbook.com/

Writing Articles from the Heart: How to Write and Sell Your Life Experiences by Marjorie Holmes. $16.99. Writer's Digest Books. http://www.writersdigest.com.

Turning Memories into Memoirs: A Handbook for Writing Lifestories by Denis Ledoux. $19.95. Soleil Press.

Writing the Memoir: From Truth to Art by Judith Barrington. $13.95. Eighth Mountain Press.

Your Life as Story: Writing the New Autobiography by Tristine Rainer. $24.95. Tarcher/Putnam.

Living to Tell the Tale: A Guide to Writing Memoirs by Jane Taylor McDonnell. $12.95. Penguin.

Aviation Books

How to Write, Publish & Sell Your Own Aviation Books by Chevy Alden. Tri-Pacer Press, PO Box 840111, Pembroke Pines, FL 33084-2111.

Biographies

Biographers and the Art of Biography by Ulick O'Connor. $28. Irish American Book Company.

Children's Books

Young at Heart: The Step-by-Step Way of Writing Children's Stories by Violet Ramos. VR Publications, vrpubs@uswest.net.

The Making of a Picture Book by Rodney Martin and John Snow. Gareth Stevens Children's Books, http://www.garethstevens.com/

Children's Writer's Word Book by Alijandra Mogilner. $19.95. Writers Digest Books. http://www.writersdigest.com.

How to Write and Illustrate Children's Books and Get Them Published edited by Treld Pelkey Bicknell and Felicity Trotman. An anthology in color. $22.50. Writer's Digest Books. http://www.writersdigest.com.

Writing for Children & Teenagers by Lee Wyndham and Arnold Madison. Writing formula for fiction and nonfiction. A revised classic. Marketing and resources. $12.95. Writer's Digest Books. http://www.writersdigest.com.

Children's Writers & Illustrator's Market (Serial) edited by Alice Pope. $19.99. Writer's Digest Books. http://www.writersdigest.com.

Writing and Illustrating Children's Books for Publication: Two Perspectives by Berthe Amos and Eric Suben. $24.95. Writer's Digest Books. http://www.writersdigest.com.

Dreams and Wishes: Essays on Writing for Children by Susan Cooper. $18. Published by Margaret McElderry.

Computer Books

How to Write Usable User Documentation by Edmond H. Weiss. $24.95. Oryx Press.

How to Write Computer Documentation for Users by Susan Grimm. $44.95. Van Nostrand Reinhold.

Cookbooks

So You Want to Write a Cookbook! by Judy Rehmel. How to collect recipes, get organized, write, print, self-publish and sell a cookbook. $6.95. Marathon International Publishing, PO Box 33008, Louisville, KY 40232.

Recipes into Type: A Handbook for Cookbook Writers and Editors by Joan Whitman and Dolores Simon. $27.50. HarperCollins.

The Recipe Writer's Handbook by Barbara Gibbs Ostmann and Jane L. Baker. $34.95. John Wiley & Sons.

Directories

Directory Publishing: A Practical Guide by Russell A. Perkins. $44.95. Cowles/Simba Information Inc. http://www.simban et.com/

Newsletter: *The Cowles/Simba Report on Directory Publishing.* Cowles/Simba Information Inc. http://www.simbanet.com/

Film/Video/TV/Stage Books

Writing Television Comedy by Jerry Rannow. http://www.allwo rth.com/

Screenwriting: Fiction and Non-fiction by Gail Kearns. For a comprehensive list of books and other resources on screenwriting, see Para Publishing's WEB Document 638 at http://ParaPublishing.com.

Top Secrets: Screenwriting by Jurgen Wolff and Kerry Cox. $21.95. Lone Eagle. 2337 Roscomare Rd. #9, Los Angeles, CA 90077-1815. Tel: (800) 345-6257; Fax: (310) 479-4969; info@loneeagle.com

How to Sell Your Screenplay by Carl Sautter. The real rules of film and television. $14.95. New Chapter Press, 381 Park Avenue South, New York, NY 10016.

Successful Scriptwriting by Jurgen Wolff and Kerry Cox. $16.99. Lone Eagle. 2337 Roscomare Rd. #9, Los Angeles, CA 90077-1815. Tel: (800) 345-6257; Fax: (310) 479-4969; info@loneeagle.com

On Screen Writing by Edward Dmytryk. Inside, hands-on scriptwriting. $24.95 ppd. Focal Press, http://books.elsev ier.com/ focalbooks/default.asp?

Television & Screen Writing: From Concept to Contract by Richard A. Blum. How-to, examples, markets and resources. $29.95. Focal Press http://books.elsevier.com/focalbooks/default.asp?

How to Write for Television by Madeline Maggio. $12. Prentice Hall. http://www.PrenHall.com

Humor Books

Comedy Writing Step by Step by Gene Perret and Carol Burnett. $11.95. Samuel French Trade. http://www.samuelfrench.com

Funny Business: The Craft of Comedy Writing by Sol Saks. $18.95. Lone Eagle Publishing. info@loneeagle.com

The Art of Comedy Writing by Arthur Asa Berger. $29.95. Transaction Publications.

Cartooning for Kids by Carol Benjamin. $14.89. HarperCollins.

Scientific/Technical/Medical Books

How to Write and Publish a Scientific Paper by Robert A. Day. $16.95. Oryx Press

Essentials for the Scientific and Technical Writer by Hardy Hoover. $7.95. Dover Publications, http://store.doverpublications.com/

Successful Scientific Writing: A Step-by-Step Guide for Biomedical Scientists by Janice R. Matthews, John M. Bowen and Robert W. Matthews. $19.95. Cambridge University Press.

A Field Guide for Science Writers: The Official Guide of the National Association of Science Writers edited by Deborah Blum and Mary Knudson. $25. Oxford University Press.

Scientific Style and Format: The CBE Manual for Authors, Editors and Publishers by Edward J. Huth. $39.95. Cambridge University Press.

Scientific English: A Guide for Scientists and Other Professionals by Robert A. Day. $19. Oryx Press.

Science as Writing by David Millard Locke. $35. Yale University Press.

How to Write and Publish Engineering Papers and Reports by Herbert B. Michaelson. $19.95. Oryx Press.

How to Write and Present Technical Information by Charles H. Sides. $19.95. Oryx Press.

Medical Writing: A Prescription for Clarity: A Self-Help Guide to Clearer Medical English by N.W. Goodman, Dr. Martin B. Edwards and Dr. Andy Black. $19.95. Cambridge University Press.

Health Writer's Handbook by Barbara Gastel, M.D. $29.95. Iowa State University Press.

Manuals

How to Write a Training Manual by John Davis. $55.95 Ashgate Publishing Co. http://www.ashgate.com/

Photo Books

Sell & Re-sell Your Photos by Rohn Engh. What sells, where to sell and pricing. Resources. $14.95. Writer's Digest Books. http://www.writersdigest.com.

Photographer's Market (Serial) edited by Donna Poehner. $23.99. Writer's Digest Books. http://www.writersdigest.com.

The Photographer's Guide to Marketing and Self-Promotion by Maria Piscopo. $18.95. Allworth Press. http://www.allwor th.com

Photography for Writers: Using Photography to Increase Your Writing Income. $18.95. Allworth Press. http://www.allwor th.com

Travel Books

Going Places, The Guide to Travel Guides by Greg Hayes and Joan Wright. *A bibliography of 3,000 travel* books. $26.95. R.R. Bowker Co., http://www.Bowker.com

Writing Travel Books and Articles by Richard Cropp, Barbara Braidwood and Susan M. Boyce. $15.95. Self-Counsel Press.

Writing Travel Articles that Sell. Three audiotapes by Gordon Burgett. $39.95. Communications Unlimited, http://www.S OPS.com

Regional Books

How to Make Big Profits Publishing City & Regional Books by Marilyn & Tom Ross. $14.95. Communication Creativity, http://www.communicationcreativity.com/index.htm

Religious Books

Writing for the Religious Market by Marvin E. Ceynar. $3.25 ppd. C.S.S. Publishing Co., http://www.csspub.com

The Complete Guide to Writing and Selling the Christian Novel by Penelope J. Stokes. $14.99. Writer's Digest Books. http://www.writersdigest.com.

Magazine Writing

Freelance Writing for Magazines and Newspapers by Marcia Yudkin. A plan for selling your work. Resources. $11. HarperCollins Publishers.

Complete Guide to Magazine Article Writing by John M. Wilson. $17.99. Writer's Digest Books. http://www.writersdigest.com.

Beginner's Guide to Writing & Selling Quality Features by Charlotte Digregorio. A simple course in freelancing for newspapers and magazines. $12.95. Civetta Press, (503) 228-6649.

Newsletter & Newspaper Writing and Publishing

Publishing Newsletters and Newsletter on Newsletters by Howard Penn Hudson. 224 pages. $39.95. H&M Publishing, Tel: (800) 572-3451; HPHudson@aol.com.

The Newsletter Handbook; How to Produce a Successful Newsletter by Wesley Dorsheimer. 194 pages, $14.95. Hippocrene Books. Tel: 201-568-5194; Tel: 201-894-5406.

Newsletter Sourcebook by Mark Beach et al.. 137 pages. $29.95. Writer's Digest Books. http://www.writersdigest.com.

Success in Newsletter Publishing; A Practical Guide by Frederick D. Goss. $39.50. Newsletter & Electronic Publishers Association, Tel: (800) 356-9302. http://www.newsletters.org

Calendar Publishing

Publishing & Marketing Your Calendar: How to Produce and Sell a Profitable Calendar by Calendar Marketing Association.

Greeting Cards

Writing Comedy Greeting Cards that Sell. Two audiotapes by Gordon Burgett. $34.95. Communications Unlimited, http://www.SOPS.com

Contracting/Legal

The Copyright Permission and Libel Handbook by Lloyd J. Jassin and Steven C. Schechter. $14.95. John Wiley & Sons.

Business and Legal Forms for Authors & Self-Publishers by Tad Crawford. Has actual tear-outs and disc with forms and contracts. $22.95. Allworth Press. http://www.allworth.com/

Publishing Agreements by Charles Clark. Sample contracts with explanations. International. $29.95. New Amsterdam Books.

Publishing Contracts on Disk by Dan Poynter. Twenty-two contracts for $29.95. Now you do not even have to type these lengthy documents. http://ParaPublishing.com

Selling Information

Writer's Market (Serial) edited by Kathryn S. BrogranKristen Holm. $27.99. Writer's Digest Books. http://www.writersdi gest.com.

How to Make a Whole Lot More than $1,000,000 Writing, Commissioning, Publishing and Selling 'How-To' Information by Jeffrey Lant. $39.95. http://www.JeffreyLant.com

The Writer's Handbook. How and where to sell magazine articles, poetry, greeting card verses, fillers, scripts and book manuscripts. An anthology of helpful chapters with a lengthy directory of resources. $30.70 ppd. The Writer; writer@kalmbach.com http://corporate.kalmbach.com/kalmbach/magazines/writer.a sp

Money for Writer$ edited by Billot. Includes grants, awards, prizes, contests, scholarships, retreats, conferences and Internet information. $19.95. Henry Holt.

The Writer's Resource Handbook by Daniel Grant. Includes career assistance, grants and awards, writers-in-residence programs, creative writing programs, legal and accounting services and insurance. $19.95. Allworth Press. http://www.allworth.com/

Getting Published: The Acquisition Process at University Presses by Paul Parsons. $33. The University of Tennessee Press, 293 Communications Building, Knoxville, TN 37996-0325. Fax: (423) 974-3724; email: jsiler@utk.edu

Book Publishing

The Self-Publishing Manual, How to Write, Print & Sell Your Own Book by Dan Poynter. The complete manual on book production, marketing and distributing. Revised edition, 432 pages. $19.95. (Para Publishing) Call 800-PARAPUB. See http://ParaPublishing.com

Financial Feasibility in Book Publishing by Robert Follett presents a step-by-step method for evaluating the financial future of new book projects. Worksheets, guidelines, projection methods, rules of thumb and estimating methods with explanations to help you decide whether your book will make money. 39 pages. $14.95 http://ParaPublishing.com

Complete Publishing Resource Manual by Linda Able. Florida Academic Press, Tel: 352-332-5104. fapress@worldnet.att.net

Self-Publishing to Niche Markets by Gordon Burgett. $14.95. Communications Unlimited. http://www.SOPS.com

How to Get Happily Published by Judith Appelbaum. How to write, find a publisher or locate an agent. $13.95. HarperPerennial.

Mastering the Business of Writing: A Leading Literary Agent Reveals the Secrets of Success by Richard Curtis. $18.95. Allworth Press. http://www.allworth.com.

The Shortest Distance Between You and a Published Book: 20 Steps to Success by Susan Page. $13. Broadway Books.

The Portable Writers' Conference: Your Guide to Getting and Staying Published edited by Stephen Blake Mettee. Great advice from more than 45 editors, agents and authors. $19.95. Quill Driver Books/Word Dancer Press, Inc., http://www.quilldriverbooks.com/default.htm

Getting Your Book Published: Inside Secrets of a Successful Author by Robert W. Bly. http://www.bly.com/

Book Proposals/Agents

How to Write a Book Proposal by Michael Larsen. Examples and resources to help you approach a publisher or agent. $14.99. Writer's Digest Books. http://www.writersdigest.com.

Nonfiction Book Proposals Anybody Can Write: How to Get a Contract & Advance Before You Write Your Book by Elizabeth Lyon. $14.95. Perigree Books

The Insider's Guide to Getting an Agent by Lori Perkins. Writer's Digest Books. http://www.writersdigest.com.

Reference books and directories

References may be used and previewed at the Reference Desk in your local public library. Write the publishers for ordering details.

From R.R. Bowker Co., 121 Chanlon Rd., New Providence, NJ 07974. Tel: (888) 269-5372. http://www.bowker.com.

Literary Market Place. Very important. Lists agents, artists, associations, book clubs, reviewers, exporters, magazines, newspapers, news services, radio and TV, and many other services. Annual. http://www.infotoday.com/

International Literary Market Place. Lists publishers, agents, suppliers, etc. in 160 countries outside the United States and

Canada. Books in Print. Lists all the books currently available by subject, title and author. Annual. http://www.infoto day.com/

Subject Guide to Forthcoming Books. A quarterly preview of *Books in Print.*

From Dustbooks, PO Box 100, Paradise, CA 95967. Tel: (800) 477-6110; Fax: (530) 877-0222; dustbooks@telis.org; http://www. dustbooks.com.

International Directory of Little Magazines and Small Presses
Small Press Record of Books in Print
Directory of Small Press/Magazine Editors & Publishers
Directory of Poetry Publishers

Magazines and Newsletters for Authors.

Small Press Review, PO Box 100 Paradise, CA 95967. Tel: (800) 477-6110; Fax: (530) 877-0222; dustbooks@telis.org; http://www.dustbooks.com.

Writer's Digest, 4700 E. Galbraith Rd., Cincinnati, OH 45236. http://www.writersdigest.com

The Writer, 21027 Crossroads Circle, Waukesha, WI 53187-1612. (800) 533-6644. writer@kalmbach.com, http://www.writermag.com

Writer's Journal, PO Box 394, Perham, MN 56573. Tel: (218-346-7921. www.writersjournal.com

Poets & Writers http://www.pw.org/

Pamphlets and reports of interest to authors.

Contact for latest prices.

National Endowment for the Arts, Literature Program, http://www.nea.gov/
Assistance, fellowships and residences for writers.

Poets & Writers http://www.pw.org/
Grants and Awards Available to American Writers
A Writer's Guide to Copyright
Writers Conferences: An Annual Guide to Literary Conferences.

Writer's Digest, 4700 E. Galbraith Rd., Cincinnati, OH 45236. http://www.writersdigest.com.
Getting Started in Writing
Jobs & Opportunities for Writers
Should You Pay to Have It Published?

P.E.N. American Center, 568 Broadway, Suite #401, New York, NY 10012. Tel: (212) 334-1660; Fax: (212) 334-2181; pen@echony.com; www.pen.org

Writers Conferences

Maui Writers Conference (Labor Day weekend). http://www.mauiwriters.com

Santa Barbara Writers' Conference (third week of June). http://www.SBWC.org

The William Saroyan Writers Conference (late March), Fresno. http://www.winwinwritersgroup.org/

Whidbey Island Writers Conference. http://www.whidbey.com/writers/

Also see http://www.ShawGuides.com/writing. http://www.quilldriverbooks.com/links/conferences.htm

Professional organizations.

Write for an application and inquire about benefits and dues. Many associations publish a magazine or newsletter. For a more complete list, see *Writer's Market*.

Mystery Writers of America
http://www.mysterywriters.org

Sisters in Crime
http://www.sistersincrime.org/

National Writers Union
http://www.NWU.org

Academy of American Poets, 584 E. Broadway, New York, NY 10012. Tel: (212) 247-0343; Fax: (212) 274-9427; http://www.poets.org

PEN American Center, 568 Broadway, Suite #401, New York, NY 10012. Tel: (212) 334-1660; Fax: (212) 334-2181; pen@echony.com; www.pen.org

Writer's Guild of America, East Chapter: 555 West 57th Street, New York, NY 10019. Tel: (212) 767-7800.
   West Chapter: 7000 W. Third Street, Los Angeles, CA 90048. Registration Tel: (213) 782-4540; www.wga.org

Authors League of America, 234 W. 44th Street, New York, NY 10036. Tel: (212) 564-8350

American Society of Journalists & Authors
http://www.ASJA.org

National Association of Science Writers
http://nasw.org/

Outdoor Writers Association of America
http://www.owaa.org/

Society for Technical Communication
http://www.stc.org

Society of American Travel Writers
http://www.WritersMarketplace.com

American Medical Writers Association
http://www.amwa.org

Garden Writers Association of America
http://www.GardenWriters.org

Horror Writers Association
http://www.horror.org

Romance Writers of America
http://www.rwanational.com

Western Writers of America
http://www.westernwriters.org/

National Writers Association
http://www.nationalwriters.com/

International Association of Business Communicators
http://www.iabc.com/

Canadian Authors Association
http://www.CanAuthors.org

Periodical Writers Association
http://www.pwac.ca/main/default.htm

Education Writers Association
http://www.ewa.org/

Web Sites for Writers

A Cappela Publishing: http://www.acappela.com

Allworth Press: http://www.allworth.com

Dick Ct's writing site
 http://www.coteliterary.com/clg_html/clg_home.html

Bookwire (links to many author web sites):
http://www.bookwire.com

Children's Writing Resource Center:
http://www.write4kids.com/index.html

Dictionary Links: http://www.yahoo.com/reference/dictionaries/

ITools! Research site: http://www.itools.com

Media Research Center: http://www.mediaresearch.org

My Virtual Reference Desk: http://www.refdesk.com/facts.html

The New York Times: http://www.nytimes.com/books

Para Publishing: http://ParaPublishing.com

Small Publishers, Artists and Writers Network (SPAWN):
http://www.spawn.org

Writers Guild of America: http://www.wga.org

Writers Net. List of agents. http://www.writers.net

http://www.write101.com

Celebrity Address Directories

Contact celebrities for testimonials. Here are the directories
we have been able to locate. Contact their publishers and look
for them at the Reference Desk of your public library.

VIP Address Book by James Wiggins. More than 30,000 names
and addresses. http://www.vipaddress.com/.

The Address Book #8, How to Reach Anyone Who Is Anyone by
Michael Levine. more than 2,500 names and addresses.
http://levinepr.com/books_address_book.html

The Ultimate Black Book by Godfrey Harris. Lists organizations
through which you can find many numbers.
http://www.AmericasGroup.com

Celebrity Bulletin, Celebrity Service Int'l, 250 West 57th Street,
Suite 819, New York, NY 10107. Tel: (212) 757-7979; Fax: (212)
956-5980

Celebrity Addresses Online. See http://www.celebrity-addresses.com
lists the home, email, etc. addresses (where known) of more than
12,000 celebrities. Also see http://people.yahoo.com/

To reach the agent of a film or TV actor, call the Screen Actors
Guild at http://www.sag.org/sagWebApp/index.jsp

Offset (Ink) printers. Contact each one for details and pricing. For information on how to draft a Request For Quotation (RFQ), see *The Self-Publishing Manual*.

Adams Press. http://www.AdamsPressChicago.com
Delta Printing Solutions, http://wwwDeltaPrintingSolutions.com
Bang Printing. http://www.bangprinting.com
Banta Information Services. http://www.banta.com
Book Mart Press (Subsidiary of Courier). http://www.cour
ier.com/ccorp/ BookMasters. http://www.bookmasters.com
C&M Press. beth@cmpress.com
C.J. Krehbiel Co. http://www.cjkrehbiel.com
Central Plains Book Manufacturing. http://www.CentralPlai
nsBook.com
Cushing-Malloy, Inc. http://www.cushing-malloy.com
Data Reproductions Corporation. http://www.datarepro.com
Dickinson Press. http://www.dickinsonpress.com
Edwards Brothers. http://www.edwardsbrothers.com
Eerdmans Printing Co. http://www.EerdmansPrinting.com
Jostens Commercial Printing. http://www.jostens.com
Jostens. booksrus@perigee.net
Malloy Incorporated. http://www.malloy.com
Maple-Vail. http://www.maple-vail.com
Marrakech Express, Inc. http://www.marrak.com
McNaughton & Gunn. http://www.bookprinters.com
Omnipress. http://www.omnipress.com
Patterson Printing. http://www.Patterson-Printing.com
Phoenix Color Corp. http://www.PhoenixColor.com
Professional Press. http://www.ProfPress.com
R.R. Donnelley & Sons. http://www.rrdonnelley.com
Rose Printing. http://www.roseprinting.com
Sheridan Books. http://www.sheridanbooks.com
Technical Communication Services. http://www.tcsbook.com
Thomson-Shore, Inc. http://www.tshore.com
United Graphics. http://www.UnitedGraphicsInc.com
Van Volumes Ltd. http://vanvolumes.com
Vaughan Printing. http://www.vaughanprinting.com
Victor Graphics http://www.victorgraphics.com
Von Hoffmann Graphics. http://www.VonHoffmann.com
Walsworth Publishing Co. http://www.walsworth.com
Whitehall Company. http://www.whitehallprinting.com

Canada

Friesen Printers. http://www.friesens.com
Gagne Printing. Tel: 819-228-2766

Hignell Book Printing. http://www.hignell.mb.ca
Tri-Graphic Printing (Ottawa-Ltd.) tgraphic@idirect.com
WebbCom Toronto. http://www.webcomlink.com

Digital Printers. See their web sites for details.

Adibooks. http://www.adibooks.com
Alexander's Digital Printing. http://www.Alexanders.com
BookJustBooks.com. http://BooksJustBooks.com
BookMobile. http://www.bookmobile.com/
C&M Press. http://www.CMpress.com
DeHart's Media Services. http://www.DeHarts.com
DigiNet Printing. http://www.DigiNetPrinting.com
Documation. http://www.documation.com/
Fidlar Doubleday. http://www.fidlardoubleday.com
Infinity Publishing. http://www.infinitypublishing.com
Morgan Printing and Publishing. mprinting@austin.rr.com
Sir Speedy Scottsdale. http://www.sirspeedy.com/Center/Loca torCentersByCity.asp
Sir Speedy-Whittier. http://www.sswhittier.com
Saint Barthlemy Books. http://www.saintbartsbooks.com/
The Document Center. http://www.xrcdti.com/
TPC Graphics. TPClen-Pat@erols.com.
Tri-State Litho. http://www.TriStateLitho.com

Colophon

This book was completely produced using the New Model production system described within.

Research and gathering
Web: MS Explorer 6.0
Art: http://www.ClipArt.com
Photos: Olympus C-50 digital camera.
Scanning: HP-ScanJet 4100-C.

Writing and manuscript building
Manuscript preparation: MS-Word

Copyediting: Melanie Rigney, http://www.editorforyou.com/

Cover design: Robert Howard of RH Graphic Design. http://www.BookGraphics.com

Design, typesetting & layout: Carolyn Porter, One on One Book Production, OneBookPro@aol.com
Page-layout program: Corel Ventura 10
Typefaces: Body text:
    NewBaskerville, 11.5 pt.
    Headers: Humanist521 BT, 10 pt.
    Chapter titles/subtitles: , Zaph Humanist, 24 pt. Bold.
    Chapter numbers: Zaph Humanist, 12 pt. Bold, italic.
    Quotations: Humanist521 BT, 11 pt. Bold.
    Stories: Myriad Roman, 10.5 pt.
    Captions: Humanists521BT 10 pt. Bold.
    Appendix: NewBaskerville 11 pt.

Conversion
MS-Word to PDF: Adobe Acrobat 6.0

Printing
Printing by McNaughton & Gunn, Ann Arbor, MI. From PDF file on disk.

Paper: 60# white offset book. 444 ppi.
Cover: 10 pt C1S, four-color, layflat film lamination.
Binding: Perfect bound (adhesive, soft-cover)

Index

Quick Order Form

⌨ **email orders:** orders@ParaPublishing.com.

📠 **Fax orders:** 805-968-1379. Send this form.

☎**Telephone orders:** Call 1(800) PARAPUB toll free (727-2782). Have your credit card ready.

🖥 **Postal orders:** Para Publishing, Dan Poynter, PO Box 8206-146, Santa Barbara, CA 93118-8206. USA. Telephone: 805-968-7277

Please send the following Books. I understand that I may return any of them for a full refund—for any reason, no questions asked.

_____

_____

_____

Please send more FREE information on:
☐Other books, ☐Speaking/Seminars, ☐Mailing lists, ☐Consulting

Name _____

Address: _____

City _____ State _____ Zip: _____-_____

Telephone:_____

email address: _____

Sales tax: Please add 7.75% for products shipped to California addresses.

Shipping by air: US: $4 for the first book or disk and $2 for each additional product. International: $9 for 1st book or disk; $5 for each additional product (estimate).

Payment: ☐Cheque, ☐Credit card:
☐Visa, ☐MasterCard, ☐Optima, ☐AMEX, ☐Discover

Card number: _____

Name on card: _____ Exp. date: ____/_____

See http://ParaPublishing.com

Para Publishing.com
Where authors and publishers go for answers

Quick Order Form

⌨ **email orders:** orders@ParaPublishing.com.

🖨 **Fax orders:** 805-968-1379. Send this form.

☎**Telephone orders:** Call 1(800) PARAPUB toll free (727-2782). Have your credit card ready.

✉ **Postal orders:** Para Publishing, Dan Poynter, PO Box 8206-146, Santa Barbara, CA 93118-8206. USA. Telephone: 805-968-7277

Please send the following Books. I understand that I may return any of them for a full refund—for any reason, no questions asked.

_____

_____

_____

Please send more FREE information on:
☐Other books, ☐Speaking/Seminars, ☐Mailing lists, ☐Consulting

Name _____

Address: _____

City _____ State _____ Zip: _____-_____

Telephone:_____

email address: _____

Sales tax: Please add 7.75% for products shipped to California addresses.

Shipping by air: US: $4 for the first book or disk and $2 for each additional product. International: $9 for 1st book or disk; $5 for each additional product (estimate).

Payment: ☐Cheque, ☐Credit card:
☐Visa, ☐MasterCard, ☐Optima, ☐AMEX, ☐Discover

Card number: _____

Name on card: _____Exp. date: ____/_____

See http://ParaPublishing.com